DELIVERING CUS

CW00595103

How To Books on business and management

Arranging Insurance
Be a Freelance Sales Agent
Buy & Run a Shop
Buy & Run a Small Hotel
Communicate at Work
Conduct Staff Appraisals
Conducting Effective Interviews
Conducting Effective Negotiations
Delivering Customer Service
Doing Business Abroad
Doing Business on the Internet
Do Your Own Advertising
Do Your Own PR
Employ & Manage Staff
Investing in People
Investing in Stocks & Shares
Keep Business Accounts
Manage a Sales Team
Manage an Office
Manage Computers at Work
Manage People at Work
Managing Budgets & Cash Flows
Managing Meetings

Managing Yourself
Market Yourself
Master Book-Keeping
Master Public Speaking
Mastering Business English
Organising Effective Training
Preparing a Business Plan
Publish a Book
Publish a Newsletter
Raise Business Finance
Sell Your Business
Selling Into Japan
Start a Business from Home
Start Your Own Business
Starting to Manage
Successful Mail Order Marketing
Taking on Staff
Understand Finance at Work
Use the Internet
Winning Presentations
Write a Report
Write & Sell Computer Software
Writing Business Letters
Your Own Business in Europe

Further titles in preparation

The How To series now contains more than 200 titles in the following categories:

Business Basics
Family Reference
Jobs & Careers
Living & Working Abroad
Student Handbooks
Successful Writing

Please send for a free copy of the latest catalogue for full details (see back cover for address).

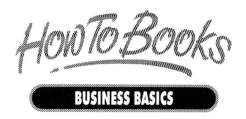

BUSINESS BASICS

DELIVERING CUSTOMER SERVICE

How to win a competitive edge through
managing customer relationships successfully

Sheila Payne

How To Books

Cartoons by Mike Flanagan

British Library Cataloguing in Publication Data
A catalogue record for this book is available from the British Library.

First published in 1997 by How To Books Ltd, 3 Newtec Place,
Magdalen Road, Oxford OX4 1RE, United Kingdom.
Tel: (01865) 793806. Fax: (01865) 248780.

Note: The material contained in this book is set out in good faith for
general guidance and no liability can be accepted for loss or expense
incurred as a result of relying in particular circumstances on statements
made in the book. The laws and regulations are complex and liable to
change, and readers should check the current position with the relevant
authorities before making personal arrangements.

Produced for How To Books by Deer Park Productions.
Typeset by PDQ Typesetting, Stoke-on-Trent, Staffs.
Printed and bound by Cromwell Press, Broughton Gifford, Melksham,
Wiltshire.

Contents

List of Illustrations

Preface

This How To Book is a practical, no-nonsense guide for all those working towards an NVQ while dealing with customers – face-to-face, in writing or on the telephone.

It explains how to maintain reliable customer service, and gives guidance on developing positive working relationships, and on how to solve problems and initiate and evaluate changes on customers' behalf. Examples and case studies help to clarify.

The contents cover the criteria for NVQ Levels 2 and 3 in Customer Service offering guidance on NVQ requirements and ways to collect and record evidence.

The book is based on many years' experience of working with customers as well as ten years teaching, assessing and counselling young people in administration and retail. Over the past three years I have assisted many candidates to achieve the NVQ Level 3 Award in Customer Service.

I would like to thank my bosses, Mick Reeve and Ann Plumbley, my work colleagues and trainees and, in particular, my daughter, Kelly Henry, for her patient proofreading.

Sheila Payne

IS THIS YOU?

NVQ candidate

Export sales clerk   Student

Teacher

Trainer   Assessor

APL adviser

Careers officer   Staff training officer

Front-line staff

Customer service manager   Customer service staff

Complaints department staff

Marketing staff   Service industry staff

Administration staff

Retail manager   Retail trainee manager

Retail assistant

Cashier   Office manager

Office supervisor

Trainee manager   Shop-floor assistant

Telephonist

Receptionist   Secretary

Charitable organisation staff

Sales representative   Tele-sales staff

Accounts staff

Garage forecourt staff   Bank clerk

Building society clerk

Post Office counter staff   Service engineer

Sales clerk

Office junior   Wordprocessing operator

Dataprocessing operator

1
Dealing with Customers

KEEPING YOUR CUSTOMERS HAPPY

Knowing the staff structure

Customers come in all shapes and sizes, all temperaments and moods. Keeping them happy isn't always easy. But no matter how you feel you have to be positive and professional at all times. If you don't know how to help a customer you should know who to go to or who to ask.

Knowing your own company structure is important. In Figure 1 you will see a simple organisation chart. If you don't have one for your company why not draw one up? Add more details than in the example so you know exactly who works in which department and what they do.

General tips to keep your customers satisfied

1. Always treat your customers courteously and with respect especially when you're working under pressure.

2. Be willing to help them and make them feel important.

3. The way you behave (chatting instead of serving, moaning instead of smiling) reflects on your company.

4. Your personal appearance also reflects on your company. Keep up your own and your company's standards at all times – try the tick-list in Figure 2 to see if you come up to scratch.

5. Make sure you have up-to-date supplies of brochures, price lists, forms and stationery available.

6. Make sure your equipment – calculator, till, computer, etc. – is in good working order and won't let you down when the customer is standing in front of you.

7. If you use a till make sure you've got enough change or arrange for a top-up before you've run out.

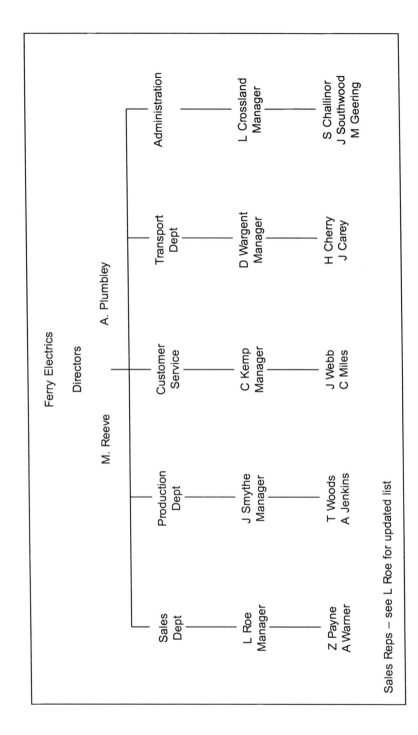

Fig. 1. Organisation chart.

8. Continually look for ways to help your customer and improve your relationships with them.

9. Don't blame your company or other staff if you can't find the information, goods or services the customer needs.

10. Always present yourself and your company positively, whether you are dealing with an existing/potential customer or another member of staff.

Do you?	Yes	No	Sometimes
Bath/shower regularly?			
Wash your hair regularly?			
Clean your teeth at least twice a day?			
Use a deodorant/anti-perspirant?			
Cut/file your nails and check they're clean?			
If you have a beard or moustache, do you regularly trim it?			
Have your hair cut regularly?			
Change your clothes each day?			
Wash and iron your clothes regularly?			
Clean and have your shoes repaired regularly?			

Fig. 2. Personal appearance tick-list.

Do unto others...?

During most weeks we all have contact with others offering us a 'service', whether it is good or bad. How many times have you had a moan about a shop assistant or thought how slow and unhelpful someone was when you telephoned about a query?

On the other hand, you may be able to think of times when a shop assistant or office worker was polite, helpful and eager to please.

Now put the boot on the other foot. You are the one offering 'service'. Which of the situations below could relate to you?

Is this you?

A customer moaned or complained that you took a long time to find information. You weren't bothered – they were only a voice on the end of the phone and would probably never ring again.

Is this you?

You dealt with a query quickly and efficiently and the customer thanked you for your help.

Customers with special needs

Some customers have handicaps which make it difficult for them to communicate with or understand you. Think of the following types of customer. How have you dealt with them in the past? Have you always treated them properly, in such a way that they leave you feeling happy and satisfied?

- Children
- Foreign visitors
- The deaf
- The blind
- The disabled
- The elderly.

Equal opportunities legislation requires us to treat everyone with the same respect and consideration. If you are not used to dealing with special problems it doesn't mean you will never come across them.

Children

If you work in a shop you probably deal with children regularly. As they are tomorrow's customers as well as today's you should treat them with as much care as you do older customers. Remember to:

- Use simple language and vocabulary.

- Help them with money and to sort out their change if necessary.

- Use their name if you know it.

- Distract them rather than rebuke them if they misbehave.

The elderly
As we get older we slow down and need a different sort of help. What the elderly don't need is to be spoken down to as though they are less than worthy of our best treatment. Remember to:

- Take your time and don't rush them.

- Avoid patronising them or speaking down to them.

- Avoid technical jargon or 'hip' words they won't understand.

- Be prepared to repeat main points again.

- Write details down if they are long and difficult to remember.

Foreign customers
Foreign customers may be even more nervous than you when they try to talk to you. They are in a strange country where most of us don't speak a second language. Remember to:

- Listen to them carefully.

- Speak slowly, use simple English words and avoid slang.

- Use short sentences only, writing key words down.

- Check you understand what they mean by repeating their words carefully.

- Avoid shouting, laughing, showing embarrassment or impatience.

- Ask for help from someone else if you are really stuck.

Physically or mentally disabled
It is very annoying for the disabled to sometimes be treated as though they are stupid rather than lacking in one of their senses. Try to forget they are disabled and concentrate on them as a person.

If they are **physically disabled** watch for signs that they need assistance. Remember to:

- Open doors for them.

- Don't rush them even if you're busy.

If the handicap is **mental**, remember to:

- Be patient and let them take their time to tell you what they want.

- Use easy-to-understand language.

The deaf
The deaf are not always easy to recognise and if they are only slightly deaf they can probably cope quite well without any problem. However, if a customer is profoundly deaf, remember to be sensitive rather than patronising. Remember to:

- Face them continually when you are speaking.

- Many deaf people can lip-read but if they can't, write down what you want to say. Keep it brief and use key words.

- Don't shout – this will distort your mouth and make lip-reading difficult.

- Use simple signs – thumbs up, for instance – to check they understand what you've told them.

The blind
The blind don't always carry a white stick. They may be partially sighted and can see a little. Remember to:

- Speak as you approach them.

- Don't grab or drag them to a chair. If they ask for help, gently guide them.

- Don't shout – they're blind, not deaf.

- Don't compare things visually, i.e. different colour shades, size, etc.

- Read information to them and ask if they would like you to repeat it.

- If they want directions to another part of the shop, office, recreation centre, etc., either take them yourself to their destination or arrange for someone else to do so if they want extra assistance.

The know-it-all
You will sometimes get a customer who knows it all – has seen it,

done it, bought the T-shirt, etc. To deal with the know-it-all you will need to keep calm. Remember to:

- Listen and try to establish what they really want.

- Explain your staff are fully qualified if they insist on telling you or them how to do their job. Thank them for their interest anyway.

- Be assertive and firm if they go on for too long.

- Be polite even when you are really busy and just want them to leave.

The customer is always right?
Well, not always. But even if they're wrong you have to bite your tongue and be subtle if they complain. Your job is to help satisfy their need. Getting angry and telling them the error of their ways is not helpful.

What do they want/need?
- They may know exactly what they want.

- They might have some idea and want your advice.

- They might not have a clue and will require close guidance.

You may have to ask yourself several things to help them:

- Do they require a product or service?

- Is the product in stock/staff available?

- Do you know where to locate the item/see who can do the job?

- Can you immediately lay your hands on the information?

- Do you know how to handle a computerised or manual stock/job allocation programme?

- What happens if you are running low/there are no staff available?

- If the item is out of stock, how do you reorder?

- Do you know where the order book is? Do you have a bookings diary?

- If a service is urgently required do you know how to check staff are available to do the job? Who do you check with before you commit the workforce?

- If the customer just wants information where do you find it?

You should know how to help them. That doesn't mean you should know all the answers.

- You might need to talk to your colleagues and ask for advice.
- Perhaps one of the staff is an expert in the particular product/ service the customer is interested in. In this case it is better to refer the customer to them.
- You may have the information in your filing system – a brochure, specialist information leaflet, instruction sheet, etc.
- If your company arranges staff training you may have learnt about a product or service which is just right for the customer's need. Refer to your notes to help the customer.

DEALING WITH PROBLEMS

Keep calm

If the customer has a problem you may not always be able to deal with it yourself. You should know which member of staff to contact and where they can be found.

If the customer is agitated and angry it isn't always easy to remain calm and think clearly. Try to remember their anger probably isn't directed at you personally.

Open and closed questioning

Ask the customer questions and listen to what they say. Watch their body language (see Chapter 3) and facial expressions. Are they saying they understand what you've told them but their face remains blank?

There are right and wrong ways to question people. Use closed questions and you'll get 'yes' and 'no' answers and nothing else. Use open questions and you'll get a better response. **Open questions** begin with:

- Why?
- When?
- How?
- Where?
- Which?
- Who?
- Can you tell me, explain, etc.?

Examples

Open questions	*Closed questions*
'Which make of video tape do you usually use?	'Is this the make you usually use?'
'Can you tell me what happened when the fault occurred?'	'You say it's not working?'

Legal rights

As well as expecting to receive courteous and helpful service, customers also have certain legal rights. Depending on the line of business you're in, different laws will affect them. You should find out about the ones you are most likely to be faced with. Below are examples of five:

- Health and Safety at Work Act
- Sale of Goods Act
- Supply of Goods and Services Act
- Trade Descriptions Act
- Financial Services Act.

Health and Safety at Work Act

We are all subject to HASAW regulations no matter what trade we are in. The purpose of the law is to ensure the safety and welfare of staff and customers in the workplace. I'm sure you've seen numerous accounts of shops and individuals being sued for damages following an accident through someone's negligence.

Example

A shop assistant has recently filled a freezer with pizzas. She didn't notice the bottom of the box was wet. Shortly after completing her task a customer slipped on the wet floor. She grasped a shelf and pulled if off the wall. A stack of tins fell on her and she was badly injured. The customer sued the shop.

Sale of Goods Act (1979)

All goods sold must comply with this Act. The person who sells the goods *not* the manufacturer is responsible. The Act states:

- The goods sold must be of a 'merchantable quality'.

- The goods must be 'fit for their purpose'.

- The goods must be as described.

Despite the Act, if you don't return the goods quickly enough, you might not get full compensation.

> *Example*
> A man bought a consignment of tiles. The colour he chose was slate grey. However, on unpacking the goods he realised they were cardinal red. He didn't return the tiles for six months. By this time the builders merchants had changed the tile supplier. He was granted a refund but not for the full amount.

Supply of Goods and Services Act

This Act relates to any goods or materials provided as part of a service or on hire. The Act states that a person providing a service must do so:

- with reasonable care and skills
- within a reasonable time (if no specific time has been agreed beforehand)
- the customer must expect to pay a reasonable charge, but if the price is agreed beforehand it cannot be queried later.

> *Note: Contracts*
> There may be penalty clauses in a contract, i.e. if a job isn't completed by a certain time your company may have to pay a 'penalty' – usually a percentage of the cost of the job. Ensure you and others are aware of any penalties as it will help to know how urgently to act if problems arise.

Trade Descriptions Act

It is a criminal offence for a trader to make false statements about any goods offered for sale. This also applies to services but only if the trader knows, or doesn't care, that he's making a misleading statement. Some traders try to get out of the Act by making disclaimer notices.

> *Example*
> A car salesman had several cars with very high mileage. He was pretty sure the clock had been turned back and to protect himself he put a notice on the car which said, 'mileage not guaranteed'.

Financial Services Act

This Act covers almost every type of investment business in this country. It doesn't apply to money invested in deposit accounts with banks or building societies.

It was introduced to help protect investors and their money. It also puts particular responsibility on the people who give advice or sell investments to customers.

What do you do about customer complaints?

How do you deal with a complaint? If you have never had a complaint it could be that you deliver such a good service that nothing ever goes wrong. Or it could be that customers merely decide never to use your services again but don't bother to tell you.

It is much better to get complaints than to hear nothing. Every dissatisfied customer will relate their experience to several others.

If you're happy to listen to complaints you satisfy the customers' needs and keep their custom. It may be your job to deal directly with the complaint or you may have to pass the customer immediately to someone else.

Whatever your company's policy . is, find out where your responsibilities are.

> **Tip**: Don't promise the customer things you may not be able to deliver. If your manager tells you later you can't give a refund or replace the article, you will look silly – and the customer may never believe a word you say again.

Refunds?

If you give service and goods away to keep a customer happy you won't be doing your company any favours. Only do this as a last resort – and with permission from a senior member of staff – if you have no other option.

There has to be a happy medium between customer and company. Use your initiative while still sticking to the rules.

MAINTAINING A GOOD SERVICE

Taking an interest in your product or service

You should know your product or service so that you can explain how something works, what its benefits are, what the advantages of having it are. You don't have to be a technical genius but you should take an interest in your product or service. How many times have you gone in a shop and asked an assistant for information and they've said they don't know?

- Read leaflets about your product or service.
- Ask questions.
- Discuss the benefits with other staff.
- Watch other more experienced staff.
- Listen to experienced staff and note what they say about a product or service.

Of course, some of the above falls a little flat if the staff member you're watching/listening to isn't very good at handling customers and dealing with queries.

Wearing the customer's shoes
Put yourself in the customer's shoes. If you feel your colleagues aren't exactly promoting the company by their attitude, don't copy them. If they are senior to you there is very little you can do about the situation other than lead by example. In other words, do your best to give good customer service. You never know, the others may copy you or management may see your good practices and arrange for training for staff who are falling short of your good example!

Updating information
It's not good enough to know your products – the ones currently in the shop, the services you offer. You also have to keep up-to-date with new lines and services as well as changes to existing ones. See Chapter 6, Keeping yourself up-to-date.

What about emergencies?
If you have a very distressed customer on the phone because they have no electricity, it's no good telling them all your electricians are busy and won't be free until next week. You have to know what to do in an emergency, who to contact and the procedures to go through.

- Can you call an engineer off one job and send him/her on another at short notice?
- How do you know where to locate him/her?
- If you don't have the authority, who does?

- How and where do you contact them?

What about stock shortages?

What happens if a regular customer has an unexpected run on an item and desperately needs more stock?

- Can you arrange a special one-off delivery that day?

- Do you have contacts with your suppliers who can rush further stocks if you run short?

- Do you have contacts with other traders who may 'lend' you stock?

- Do you charge extra for a special delivery?

The only way to maintain a good service to your customers is to take an interest in your job and find out what makes it tick. Don't rely on others to tell you, find out for yourself.

COLLECTING EVIDENCE FOR YOUR NVQ

If you are working towards an NVQ you will need to collect evidence to prove you give good customer service. The examples you collect may be suitable for cross-referencing against other Elements in the Customer Service Award.

Below are a few examples of the types of evidence you can use. The list is for guidance only and you may have other items which will be just as appropriate. The list covers the following Elements:

Customer Service Level 2
Element: 1.1   1.2   3.1

- Examples of brochures and information leaflets on your product/ service.

- Letters from customers thanking you for your help.

- Copy of job allocation chart, work schedule, bookings diary or a similar book or form which shows where staff are and what job they're on.

- Memos or notes from other staff asking you to deal with a customer.

- A flow chart to show the channels you need to go through to resolve a problem when things go wrong.

- An organisation chart of your company showing where staff fit into the team.

- Minutes of meetings where your name is mentioned as delivering good customer service.

- Your job description showing what your duties and responsibilities are.

- A case study showing how you dealt with a particular problem (see Chapter 9).

- Witness statements from colleagues and customers.

CHECKLIST

Below are 'user friendly' checklists for the NVQ Performance Criteria. You will find the appropriate Elements at the end of each chapter. Use them to see where you need more experience or training to meet the standards of the Level 2 or 3 Customer Service Award.

Level 2 Element 1.1 **Deliver products or services to customer:**

Performance criteria	Can do	Need more experience	Need training
(a) Can you supply your company's products or services quickly when asked?			
(b) Can you suggest other products and services if you can't supply what they want?			
(c) Can you sensitively question your customer to find out exactly what they want?			
(d) Do you continually update your own knowledge of the products or services you supply by using company information?			

Level 2 Element 1.2 **Maintain service when systems go wrong**

Performance criteria	Can do	Need more experience	Need training
(a) Can you immediately explain to your customers why you can't supply a service?			
(b) Do you keep your customers up-to-date if a service is interrupted?			
(c) Does the information you give to customers protect them from unnecessary worry?			
(d) Do you make extra effort to maintain a good service when things go wrong?			
(e) Do you help your colleagues and offer them practical help when things go wrong?			

Level 2 Element 3.1 **Present positive personal image to customer**

Performance criteria	Can do	Need more experience	Need training
(a) Are you always courteous and helpful, especially when you're under pressure?			
(b) Do you always maintain a good personal appearance and behave in a responsible manner?			
(c) Do you make sure the equipment you use in your job is in good working order? Is your paperwork, literature, stationery, etc. up to date?			
(d) Do you take any opportunity you can to improve working relationships with customers?			
(e) Do you present a positive image of yourself and your organisation to customers and colleagues?			

CASE STUDIES – INTRODUCTION

All the characters in the following case studies work for the same Hampshire-based activity centre. No matter what their job role involves, one thing is common to all – good customer service.

At least three of the characters will be involved in each chapter.

Virginia Plain – Bookings Co-ordinator

Virginia is twenty-five and has worked for a busy activity centre in Hampshire for five years. She enjoys her work, understands the importance of good customer service and gets on well with both staff and customers.

The centre itself has accommodation for one hundred and forty visitors as well as tented accommodation for two hundred. Her role is to co-ordinate bookings, ensure there is sufficient and appropriate accommodation available as well as liaise with programme staff for daily and weekly courses. Communication between the Programme Director, groundsmen, activity, kitchen and cleaning staff is vital to ensure the weekly programme runs smoothly and the accommodation is ready when the groups arrive.

She also deals with the customers including school heads, teachers, youth and church leaders, company managers, caravan and camping organisers, training officers and the visitors themselves on arrival.

Bryan Houghton – Programme Director

Bryan is thirty-five. He lives in the grounds of the activity centre and has been there for eight years.

In his role as Programme Director he liaises with customers, programme staff, the Bookings Co-ordinator and outside agencies (riding stables, sailing clubs, trips to places of interest, etc.) ensuring they take into consideration what the customer wants and deliver it as safely as possible. It is essential he checks the programme is staffed effectively and that any outside activity is booked and transport to-and-from arranged.

Although he organises the programme well he is unpopular with the centre staff, in particular the activity staff. He tends to favour one or two of his favourites giving them the best programme and most popular groups while ignoring the feelings, needs or wants of the majority of the other staff. This leads to some resentment which is sometimes picked up by the customer.

Lee Henry – Activity Instructor

Lee is twenty-six and moved from his native Wales a year ago to live on-site at the activity centre. He now dates Carina, one of the other activity staff. He is an experienced instructor in archery, canoeing and orienteering and has a clean driving licence. He shares a room with two other members of the activity staff.

Lee's day is long – he rises early to accompany new groups to breakfast – it is part of his job-role to help clients settle in and ensure that meal-times are part of the enjoyable experience of their week's stay. He is a natural comedian and popular with visitors. During the day he takes activity sessions as well as driving visitors to the riding stables several miles away. In the evenings he is also involved in team-building activities, trekking and bivouacking, etc.

His time off is spent at the centre as he has no transport of his own. Occasionally he walks to the local village or, if Carina is off at the same time, they will catch a bus or train into town.

The Programme Director and Lee don't see eye-to-eye. They have had more than one confrontation since Lee's arrival. Lee's mood after such a confrontation tends to be rather black. He finds it hard to separate the feelings of anger and resentment from his professional side.

Kelly Chinn – Receptionist

Kelly is seventeen and on a government training scheme. She lives in the local village with her parents. She has been the centre's receptionist for eighteen months and was trained by the Bookings Co-ordinator, Virginia, who is now her mentor.

Kelly's duties include greeting visitors, issuing room keys, supplying change for vending machines, answering the telephone and keeping a log of calls, receiving and distributing mail, keying-in information into the computer, giving out information to visitors and taking money when they pay their bill. She tries to keep everyone happy but knows when she can't cope. If Reception is too busy for one person she enlists the help of one of the other office staff who are in a connecting room.

DISCUSSION POINTS

1. Can you think of two situations when you were thanked for helping a customer? What do you think you did particularly well to warrant the thanks?

2. How do you keep your own knowledge of your products or services up-to-date?

3. Have you had a customer complaint which wasn't resolved? If so, what would you do differently if a similar situation arose in the future?

2
Keeping Records

WHY KEEP RECORDS?

Record-keeping is of vital importance if you want to improve your service to customers. If they telephone with a query or complaint you should be able to immediately find their file/data record and deal with the problem.

If you can't help them you should transfer them to someone else or take a message and make sure it gets passed to the right person (see Figure 3).

MESSAGE FORM

TO:................................... DEPT:............................

DATE: .... TIME:.............................

CALLER'S NAME: ....

COMPANY: ....

TEL NO: .... EXT:.............................

Telephoned ☐

Returned your call ☐

Called to see you ☐

Left a message ☐

Please return call ☐

Please arrange appointment ☐

Message: ....

....

....

....

....

Taken by: .... Dept: ....

Fig. 3. Message pad.

Keeping basic records

Basic records should be kept on all customers with additional or unusual information in note form. For instance, on a computer database or card index the following are the basis for the record:

- customer name, address, telephone and fax number

- what services/goods they usually buy from you

- whether they are a priority customer

- how they pay (cash, cheque, or have they been authorised to book the goods or services on credit)

- any agreed discount

- any problems they've had or complaints they've made

- if they're good payers/owe you money

- if they are on a blacklist and should be refused credit.

Sales feedback

Today, marketing is an increasingly important part of any business. Accurate records can help you see what services or goods are most popular, which seasons have the most demand for certain things and what causes a customer to complain.

If a book or log is kept with these details it can help to improve your service and predict which months you may need to buy extra stock or employ additional staff. It will also help you highlight complaints which crop up again and again.

Knowing your filing system

You should know what systems exist in your company and how to use them. Only by using them can you know if the system is efficient and serves the purpose of the job. (See Figure 4.)

Manual storage system

This can consist of a small card index box or a larger box file. It may be a whole filing cabinet or row of storage cupboards. (See Figure 5.)

Checklist

Use the checklist on page 32 to find out the things you should know about your filing system. If you ticked any as 'don't know' find out the answer from someone who does.

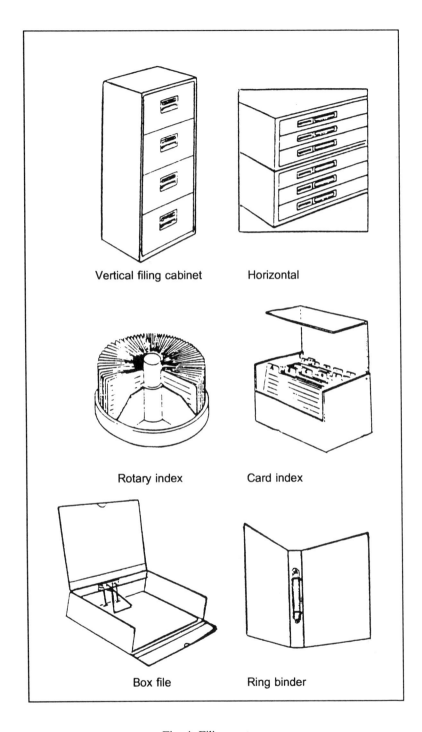

Vertical filing cabinet   Horizontal

Rotary index   Card index

Box file   Ring binder

Fig. 4. Filing systems.

Name: *HEPBURN, SAMANTHA*

Company: *PREMIER PROMOTIONS*

Address: *24 BRIARWOOD CLOSE*

BISHOP'S WALTHAM SO32 2NA

Tel No: *01489 896130*   Fax No: *01489 896170*

E Mail No: ....

Additional Info: ....

....

Continue on back of card if necessary.

Fig. 5. Manual customer record card.

Computerised filing system

A computerised filing system is only as good as the people operating it. If it is your job to update the information, check it carefully for errors once it has been entered. (See Figure 6.)

Business Contacts

Date Entered: 28.9.9-   (the date you entered data in this form)

Mr./Mrs./Ms.: Mr

First Name: Andrew   Last Name: Dijken

Company: Ferry Electrics

Address Line 1: Admiral House
Address Line 2: 67 High Street

Town: Fareham   County: Hampshire

Postal Code: PO16 7BB   Country: England

Phone: 01329 825805   Fax: 01329 825608

| Credit Limit: | | Account Rating: | 3 |
| No of Outlets: | | 2 | |

Fig. 6. Computerised data record.

	Yes	No	Don't know

Do you store information:
  alphabetically (by the alphabet)?
  numerically (by numbers)?
  alphanumerically (by the alphabet
  and numbers)?
  chronologically (by dates)?
  subject order (by the subject)?
  geographically (by town, county,
   country)?			

Do you have a special filing tray?			
Do you file every day/once a week?			
What about documents you don't know where to file? Who do you ask to find out?			
Where do you file – in a suspension, box, card index file, lever arch, wallet, concertina file?			
Is the latest information put at the front or back of the file?			
Do you always check to make sure you have filed the document in the right place?			
Does someone else do the filing? If so, where is their filing tray?			
What happens if you want to open another file?			
If you think of a better system to file papers who would you go to for permission to introduce it?			
What about confidentiality? What is your company's policy on this?			
What do you do with out-of-date information?			
Do you know how long information should be kept – for both legal and company purposes?			

Computerised storage system checklist

	Yes	No	Don't know

Do you store data:
   under a name?
   under a code?
   under a number?			

Do you have a special tray for documents which have to be entered onto the database?			
Do you enter data every day/once a week?			
Where do you place documents once information has been entered into your system?			
Do you proofread (check for errors) your work carefully?			
Do you print out the data on completion?			
Does someone else enter the data? If so, where is their data collection tray?			
What happens if you want to open another datafile?			
What do you do with out-of-date data files? Where are data disks/tapes stored?			
Do you know about the Data Protection Act?			

RETURNS DIARY	
Date of Return	File Name
23.7.9-	*C and L Ross*
23.7.9-	*R Houghton Furnishings*
24.7.9-	*GHA*
24.7.9-	*Wargent Photographic*

Return cards

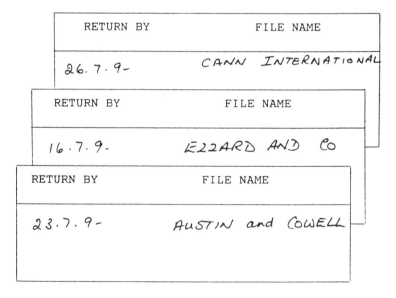

Fig. 7. Returns diary and return card.

IMPROVING YOUR FILING SYSTEM

To improve your filing system you must try to streamline it. Hold up-to-date information and clear out old clutter once it's of no further use. However, don't throw it away (see information on 'dead files'). Keep a track on where files are – if they're missing it can be as frustrating as not having any information at all.

File movements
What happens when you urgently need a borrowed file? You have two options:

• Ask everyone in the office.

• Search on desks and in other filing cabinets (in case it's been wrongly filed).

Returns diary and return card
There is a way to track a file – an 'out' card could be placed in the empty file. Even a piece of scrap paper with the borrower's name, department and date would be sufficient.

Some larger companies keep a returns diary with the files listed under the date of return. Entries are crossed out when they've been returned.

Another system is to have a card index book just for borrowed files. The cards are dated when the file is due for return. The card is removed when the file is returned, leaving cards with outstanding files still in the box. (See Figure 7.)

Removing information from the system
If staff are in the habit of taking out the suspension file as well as the information inside, a file can go missing for a while before it's noticed.

> **Tip**: If you place the information inside a manila folder, the suspension file is still in place when the information has been borrowed. The empty file will highlight the missing information.

Getting the other staff into the habit of taking only the cardboard file and using the system of a returns diary or 'out' cards will be your biggest problem. Anything new has its teething problems, but it's well worth the effort to try to implement the system.

KEEPING UP-TO-DATE RECORDS

It's no good having a filing system where recent information hasn't been filed or put onto computer. It's also important that the information stored is easy to read and correct.

Key points to remember about keeping and maintaining records

- Know your system. What is the easiest and quickest way to access the information? Is it from the card index box, the manual file or computer?

- Keep your own notes for information that you're asked for regularly. Don't retrace your steps to the same old file week after week.

- The records must be correct and contain all the relevant details and facts relating to the subject.

- The facts should be set out clearly without any unnecessary information getting in the way.

- You should regularly check the records to ensure they are still up-to-date and correct. Out-of-date telephone numbers and addresses are just one cause of lost time and money.

- If you think of a way to improve the system suggest this to the correct person who makes the decision to change systems.

- If you have made authorised changes to the system make sure the other staff know how it works.

Confidential information

Your customers and other staff have rights regarding confidential information they give you. You should ensure that:

- confidential files are kept locked in a separate cabinet

- they are only made available to people with proper authority to read them

- they are never left lying on a desk.

Data Protection Act

The Data Protection Act 1984 has strict guidelines to ensure that confidential information entered on computers isn't used in the wrong way. In brief, it states:

- If you hold employee data on computer you must register as a data user.

- The information you hold must be obtained legally.

- Personal data must not be given to other people.

- All data must be kept up-to-date and be accurate.

- Companies must ensure that unauthorised access, alteration or destruction of data is not permitted.

- Personal records must not be kept any longer than necessary.

Practical filing

The system must be kept up-to-date and if this is done regularly it will soon become a habit. As long as everything is filed in the correct place paperwork will be easy to find when a customer telephones with an enquiry.

All papers should be kept in good condition. Papers soon become torn and creased if they are forced into an overcrowded file.

> **Tip**: To keep important documents clean and tidy you can place each one in a plastic wallet, but these shouldn't be used for everyday letters and documents as they can be expensive. Cheaper cardboard files, manila or wallet folders (see Figure 8) are another way of keeping papers in good order.

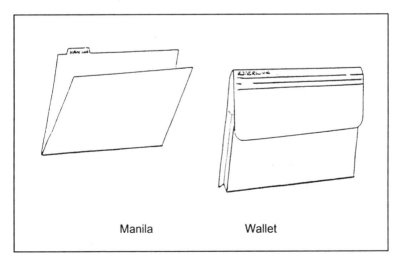

Manila   Wallet

Fig. 8. Folders.

What's a dead file?

If you kept every document for an eternity you would soon disappear under a mountain of paper. Every so often you should go through the files and store out-of-date papers elsewhere. These are classed as 'dead'.

Don't throw documents away. Store them safely in a **dead file**. A dead file doesn't have to be a special file; it can be either a box or large envelope, new or secondhand. Make sure you mark the outside of the container with large, clear letters so you can find the information again. Store them in the loft, store cupboard, cellar – wherever there's a spare space.

> **Remember**: Don't store them where they may be a health and safety hazard, i.e. where they could contribute to a fire or health hazard.

How old should papers be before I ditch them?

Use the following as a guide:

Item	Keep for
Ordinary business correspondence	One or two years
Accounts and VAT documents	Minimum of six years (required by law)
Legal documents	Minimum of six years
Important documents	Should be kept indefinitely

QUICKLY FINDING INFORMATION

If you receive a letter from a customer with a query or complaint you are under less pressure than if they are on the phone or standing in front of you. You still need to sort the problem quickly but don't have the eyes and ears of your customer demanding immediate attention.

If the query is from another member of staff you are under a different sort of pressure. They will probably want the information for a different purpose – to answer their own customer query, to produce an annual report, to update their own files, etc.

Speeding up the search

When you are under pressure remember the following to help speed up the process:

- Make sure you understand exactly what information is needed.

- Think carefully about where you can get the information. It should be by the easiest and quickest route available:
  - from the files
  - from the computer
  - from another person
  - from your own notes.

- Quickly collect all the information available. If you can't find it think of alternative ways to supply what's required.

- Return to the customer/member of staff and explain any problems you've had. Offer alternative information if it is appropriate.

- When all the information has been collected, sort it out and decide how best to give it to the customer/member of staff:

  Quickest route
  Photocopied or written
  Copies of leaflets or brochures collected and put together
  Printout from computer

  If you have more time
  Typed or wordprocessed in the form of a report, letter or memo
  Displayed in graph or spreadsheet
  Displayed in columns (tabular).

- Don't give confidential information to anyone who hasn't got the authority to have it.

Copyright, Designs and Patents Act 1988

© = Copyright Act. It is illegal for you to make a copy of published books and other literature carrying the Copyright symbol. Most educational organisations are granted a licence, upon payment of a fee, for schools and colleges to make limited copies. Copies can be made for research and study but remember you and your organisation can be prosecuted if you abuse the Act. Any library will have a copy of the Act if you want further information.

Example
Police picked up a market trader in Portsmouth. He was selling

boot-leg film videos he'd copied himself. He was prosecuted for contravening the Copyright Act.

COLLECTING EVIDENCE FOR YOUR NVQ

Below are a few examples of evidence you can collect for the following NVQ Elements.

Customer Service Level 2   **Level 3**
Element: 2.1   2.2   **Element: 1.1**

- Copy of card index – blank or with imaginary details if the information is confidential.

- Copy of database printout – blank or with imaginary details if the information is covered by the Data Protection Act.

- Brochures and leaflets you use to help with customer queries.

- Your notes on information you've been asked to collect from the files.

- Reports, graphs, tables, letters and other ways of displaying information you've collected (delete confidential information).

- A flow chart to show how you collected a piece of information (request given, plan where to search, search files, collect information, plan how to present it, draft copy, final copy).

- A copy of your company's policy on the Data Protection Act, the Copyright laws, confidentiality.

- Copy of company annual report if you've helped collect information for it.

- A case study.

- Witness statements from colleagues/customers.

CHECKLIST

Level 2 Element 2.1　　　　　　　**Maintain an established storage system**

Performance criteria	Can do	Need more experience	Need training
(a) Do you follow your organisation's procedures to put new information into the manual or computer system of filing?			
(b) Do you keep the materials you store in good condition and put them in the right place?			
(c) Do you check where the files are and who's got them? Do you record it somewhere?			
(d) Do you know when a file is missing? Do you know what to do to make sure it's returned?			
(e) Do you follow instructions on dealing with out-of-date information?			
(f) Can you think of ways to improve your storage system? What actions would you take to carry out the improvements?			
(g) Do your work practices conform to your organisation's requirements?			

Level 2 Element 2.2   **Supply information for a specific purpose**

Performance criteria	Can do	Need more experience	Need training
(a) If you're asked for information, do you ask for more details if you don't understand what's wanted?			
(b) Can you identify where to get information from and then get it quickly?			
(c) If you can't find what's wanted, can you think of other ways to get the required information?			
(d) Can you put all the information together so it makes sense?			
(e) Can you supply the information in the correct form – in a tabular, graphical or textual form (see Chapter 6 for more details)?			
(f) Can you supply the information within required deadlines?			
(g) Do you ensure confidential information is only disclosed to those who have authority to see it?			

Level 3 Element 1.1 Maintain records relating
to customer service

Performance criteria	Can do	Need more experience	Need training
(a) Do the documents you keep contain all the relevant facts? Are they correct, clear, complete and comprehensive?			
(b) Can you set out the facts clearly and in an easy-to-understand way when preparing records?			
(c) Do you regularly and accurately check, update and correct your records?			
(d) Are any suggestions you make to improve the record system based on your customers' needs?			
(e) Are any suggestions you make to improve the record system passed on to the correct authority?			
(f) Can you clearly recognise which records can be used to monitor the delivery of customer service?			
(g) Can your records be easily retrieved by others?			
(h) Do your records conform to statutory regulations and requirements regarding confidentiality, e.g. Data Protection Act?			

CASE STUDIES

Virginia gets computerised

Virginia Plain's company has recently bought a networked computer system to be used by the Bookings and Programme Departments. The reception area is also to have a linked terminal.

She has decided to get the old manual customer record system transferred to computer. Details will only be entered by herself or Kelly Chinn, the Receptionist, during quiet times during the day. She is aware of how important accuracy will be.

Bryan tries to help

Bryan Houghton decides he wants to be involved in setting up the system. He tells two of his activity staff they are to help key-in the information. They have no experience of using computers or working in an office and resent being asked. Bryan informs them they will have to do what they're told as he has written it into their work schedule.

Kelly corrects the errors

Kelly Chinn was hoping to input quite a bit of data into the computer during an exceptionally quiet morning. The centre is so busy at the moment it is a rare occasion. Unfortunately, she is unable to get very far as most of her time is spent correcting errors made by the activity staff.

She doesn't blame the activity staff but is frustrated at the time she has wasted in correcting their errors. Because her supervisor is away and she's aware the activity staff have been scheduled to use the computer that afternoon, she asks Bryan Houghton if he would mind taking them off their office duties. He reminds her she is only a trainee and criticises her for challenging him. She bites her lip and returns to Reception.

DISCUSSION POINTS

1. What are your company's policies on length of time to keep certain documents? Where are dead (out-of-date) files stored before they are disposed of?

2. Can you think of a way to speed up the supply of information? Does this involve changing the system you currently use?

3. Who would you go to if you thought of a better way to use the filing system? What would you have to do to get the system officially recognised?

3
Another Satisfied Customer

NOTICING NON-VERBAL SIGNALS

Signals to watch for
There is no real mystery to reading non-verbal signals and to show how easy it is, below is a small exercise. There are four actions and beside them four descriptions of behaviour. See if you can match them up:

Match the action	With the description
(a) A customer is fiddling with their bag and seems reluctant to approach the counter.	(1) Angry
(b) A visitor has arrived in Reception while you're dealing with another customer. They begin to tap the desk to get your attention.	(2) Pleasant
(c) A customer is taking their time to choose an item from a tray you are holding. Another customer is glaring at you while he's waiting.	(3) Nervous
(d) A customer smiles warmly as they approach your desk.	(4) Impatient

Answers
(a) = (3)   (b) = (4)   (c) = (1)   (d) = (2)

Why signals are important
Understanding that actions speak louder than words enables you to see beyond the initial contact with a customer.

- It helps you to vary your own behaviour to ensure you don't antagonise the customer or make matters worse if there's a problem.

- When a customer is nervous or embarrassed, if you handle the situation properly they will tell you what they want instead of walking out of the shop or office empty-handed.

An introduction to unspoken communication

There are many ways to judge how someone is feeling. The following is a small introduction to the world of silent communication.

Standing or walking

Shifting	Moving from one foot to the other means the person is feeling uncomfortable. They may feel excluded if they are in a group.
Hands in pockets	Could mean the person's cold! But if they're standing, it could also mean they are secretive and withdrawn. They can be critical of others but give little or nothing personal about themselves away.
Leaning	This is way of relaxing while standing. We seem to find it difficult to stay vertical for long periods.
Head bowed	If a person walks with hands in pockets and their head bowed it could indicate depression. The person will often kick small objects – or even imaginary ones – while walking.
Folded arms	Some women walk with arms folded, especially if walking alone – this is a defensive pose and one that tells you the person is feeling vulnerable.
Strutting	The person walks with rigid arm movements, the chin is raised giving a superior look. It indicates a person is arrogant, self-centred with fixed opinions.

Eye movement

Thinking	Eyes closed for a time during a conversation could mean the person is trying to remember something more clearly.

Exasperated	Eyes closed for a time during a conversation while the person draws breath and sighs heavily could mean the person is fighting for control over something which is causing them irritation or annoyance.
Evasive	Staring sightlessly into the air or down at the ground. Unable to look you in the eye. There may be a conversation but the person is avoiding the issue.
Shifty	Rapidly glancing to and fro. They look you in the eye quickly, then look away. They are searching for an exit.

Hand signals

Clenched	If the hands are clenched when speaking it indicates someone is frustrated or in pain. If they are listening, hand clenching is a negative response.
Pointing	Using the index finger to point at someone when they are talking indicates they want to dominate, are aggressive and authoritarian.
Head scratching	This indicates they are confused or uncertain about what is being said. They're not sure how to take the information.
Clasping	Clasping the back of the neck often means the person is trying to control angry feelings. It could mean an argument is brewing.
Pressed	Hands flat and pressed together indicates the person is demonstrating the desire to persuade or underline a point.

Facial expressions

Figure 9 gives some examples of different facial expressions and the moods or feelings they probably reflect.

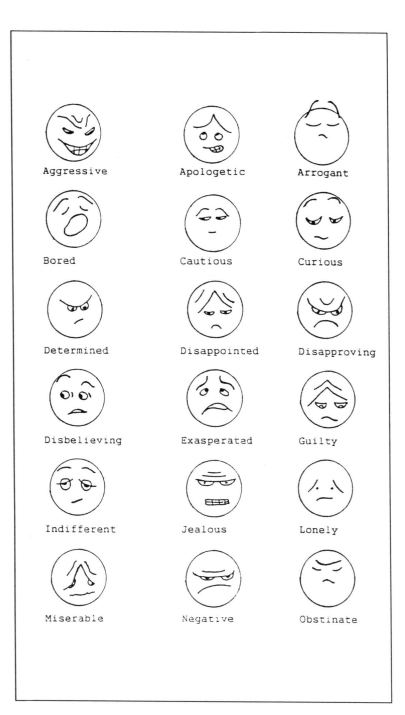

Fig. 9. Non-verbal facial expressions.

Faking a complaint

How do you spot if a customer is lying about a complaint? The first three signs in the list below can be confusing because they are the same as someone who has had an argument and has been wrongly accused.

1. Liars find it difficult to look you in the eye. They will look down, look away or glance at you briefly if at all. Experts can tell the state of a person's emotions by the way their pupils dilate.

2. They will have a dry mouth and will lick their lips more often.

3. They will probably swallow more often because they are frightened of being exposed.

4. They may clear their throat more often than usual.

5. Their breathing may become more uneven.

6. They may cross their legs and arms simultaneously.

7. Their feet could be facing towards the door – in case they need to make a hasty exit.

8. Their posture is often stiff and controlled. As they are holding back the truth their honest physical expression is also being held back. This may prompt body shifts – children squirm when they are being dishonest.

9. They may scratch, rub or stroke their nose more than someone who is being straightforward.

10. Ignore the content of speech and concentrate on how the words are being spoken. The normal voice flattens, loses its depth and becomes more monotonous because the liar is holding back from freely expressing themselves. They make mistakes in their speech and are more likely to stutter, slur or hesitate as they speak.

PACIFYING AN ANGRY OR NERVOUS CUSTOMER

Calming them down

If the customer or caller is feeling angry and aggressive you will have to calm them before you can help resolve the problem:

- Be polite and patient.

- Don't interrupt but listen carefully.

- If you know you can't help them, get someone who can.

If the customer or caller is shy or nervous:

- Smile and try to put them at their ease.

- Don't interrupt but listen carefully.

- Give the information they need slowly and quietly.

- If you feel they haven't understood, repeat the information if necessary.

Questioning

Sometimes the non-verbal signals given by a customer aren't always that easy to work out. You may need to ask them questions as well as judge their outward appearance (see Chapter 1, open and closed questions).

Be sensitive and watch their reactions when you question them, changing the line of questioning if you see them become more confused, anxious or aggressive.

Trying to clarify the situation for them

- Write the details down.

- Hand out brochures or leaflets and explain their content.

- Ask if the customer wants more information.

- Check you've answered their query or whether they still have unanswered questions.

- Check their non-verbal signals – are they saying they're OK, but their face tells you they're still confused?

- Adapt your next action depending on the above point.

KEEPING YOUR COOL

Keeping stress under control

When things go wrong, they seem to go wrong in pairs – or even in threes. Sometimes you may feel as though you are under personal attack and if anything else goes wrong you'll scream. But it isn't stress itself that causes problems – it's an excess of stress.

Causes of stress

- One thing goes wrong and then another. The third thing, although relatively small, sends you over the top.

- People demand too much of you, asking you to do things when you are already overstretched.

- You're trying to prepare an important report or put an urgent order together, and the other staff keep talking to you. Worse still, they talk and joke to each other as though they have nothing to do while you are stretched to the limit.

- You have a personal problem or don't feel well. You don't want sympathy or time off but you're finding it hard to act your normal happy self.

- There don't seem to be enough hours in the day and as the clock's hand reaches 4.30 pm you still haven't finished all the jobs you know you have to do.

Ways of tackling stress and keeping your cool
- Find out what's causing the problem – work overload, arguments with work colleagues, personality clash with someone you work with or for, changes in your life (death in the family, divorce, redundancy, etc.), problems at home, etc.

- Face up to the problem and decide why you find the situation stressful, who or what is involved, what you can or can't do about it, what you want to do about it.

- Decide what you can do about the problem. You might decide to sort out your work schedule or talk to the person you feel badly about. You could approach a senior member of staff and talk about it or even go on an assertiveness course to help you deal with people who are putting on you.

- If you decide there's nothing you can do, the problem may continue. If it's a death or personal tragedy try to think of ways to distract yourself:
  – give yourself a treat
  – take up a hobby
  – cuddle something even if it's only the neighbour's dog
  – plan a special outing
  – tell yourself how lucky you are in other areas.

If you are merely feeling sorry for yourself and decide nothing will help, you should rethink the problem. Is it really as bad as you seem to think it is? Is there really nothing you can do to solve it? There's usually an answer to every problem if you give it some extra thought.

Use the quiz in Figure 10 to work out your own liability to stress.

Statement	Always	Sometimes	Never
I am never late			
I live for my job			
I eat quickly			
I am impatient			
I play to win			
I am ambitious			
I rarely show my feelings			
I talk rapidly			
I am usually in a hurry			
I feel guilty when I am not working			

Always   = 2 points
Sometimes   = 1 point
Never   = 0 point

According to Americans Friedman and Rosenman (who conducted research to isolate two main types of personality) the quiz indicates:

High scores = Type A personality who will experience considerable
(over 16)   stress

Low scores   = Type B personality who are more easy-going and less
(under 8)   likely to suffer from stress

Type A are more likely to climb to the top but are also prone to heart disease and heart attacks.

Fig. 10. Stress quiz.

SORTING OUT CUSTOMER COMPLAINTS

If you've had 'one of those days' and you're feeling stressed, the last thing you want to deal with is a customer complaint. But it won't go away. You have to tackle it head on.

Take a deep breath

Don't let the situation get out of control by shouting back if you feel you're under attack from a customer. Instead, let them finish and rid themselves of all the pent-up anger. Now take a deep breath and think carefully before speaking:

- Stay calm.

- Pacify them.

- Be sympathetic but don't accept the blame on behalf of your company or a colleague.

- Be as reasonable, patient and helpful as you can.

- Take written note of what the customer is saying. This will show you are doing something positive.

- Assure the customer you will follow up the problem and get back to them.

You may have to sort things out there and then if the customer refuses to leave the premises or insists on hanging on if they're speaking to you on the telephone. Do this immediately or get a more senior member of staff to talk to them. The situation will only worsen if you make them wait.

Your complaints procedure

What is the correct way to deal with a complaint in your company? If you don't know, find out. Draw a flow chart to show the stages – this can be used as part of your evidence if you are working towards an NVQ. See the example on page 54.

Admitting your own mistakes

If you ask for help and the problem is due to a mistake you've made, denying the fact to your work colleagues may make you feel even more defensive and agitated.

Example of a complaints procedure

Customer complains
↓
If it's about faulty goods I examine them
↓
If there's an obvious flaw I replace them
or offer a credit
↓
I write all details in the feedback log
↓
If there's no obvious flaw I call my supervisor
↓
If it's about faulty service I get the details
↓
If I can't deal with it I contact my supervisor
↓
If it's a complaint about a member of staff
I pass it immediately to my manager

- Admit mistakes – we all make them so don't try to blame someone else or deny it's your fault. As long as you learn from the experience no one will shoot you at dawn.

- Once you've accepted responsibility, do something positive to sort things out.

- If you need help from another member of staff, admit in full the mistakes you've made.

- If someone else has made a mistake, don't blame or criticise them (*never* do this in front of the customer). Ask them to help solve the problem.

Company responsibility

You should never promise the customer the earth in order to please them. You have a responsibility to your company as well as the customer.

To get a good balance between what the customer needs and what your company can deliver remember the following:

- If the customer makes a complaint find out exactly what they expect from you and your company.

- Decide whether they are being realistic in their demands and whether you have the authority and power to sort things out on your own. Don't attempt to make decisions which you know are not your responsibility or within your authority.

- Speak clearly and positively when you explain any limitations your company have set you. These could involve costs, time and resources you have available.

- If it isn't in your power to help the customer pass them on to someone who can make higher decisions – your manager or another more senior member of staff.

- Once a decision has been made make a record of it – even if it's only a small note attached to the customer's file or a brief entry on the database.

Is a customer complaint good for your company?

Customers who have made complaints and have been dealt with properly and to their satisfaction often become very valuable to a company. Their word-of-mouth praise about the help they've received will act as good publicity.

COLLECTING EVIDENCE FOR YOUR NVQ

Listed below are a few examples of evidence you can collect for the following NVQ Elements:

Customer Service Level 2
Element: 3.2   3.3   3.4

- Examples of brochures and information leaflets on your product/ service.

- Letters from yourself to customers introducing them to new products or services.

- A copy of your company's Equal Opportunities/Non-discriminatory policy.

- Flow chart showing complaints procedure.

- Customer complaints log.

- Customer complaints in writing with the reply to prove you've sorted out the problem.

- Minutes of meetings where your name is mentioned as delivering good customer service.

• A case study.

• Witness statements from colleagues/customers.

CHECKLIST

Level 2 3.2   **Balance needs of
                                        customer and organisation**

Performance criteria	Can do	Need more experience	Need training
(a) Do you make a real effort to meet your customer's needs within the limits of your own authority?			
(b) Do you clearly and positively explain the company limitations you are under if you can't give the customer exactly what they are demanding?			
(c) Do you do everything you can to help your customer while minimising the conflict between what they want and what your company can deliver?			
(d) When you reach the organisation's limits of what you can do to help your customer, do you seek help and assistance from others?			
(e) Do you record and store the details of your dealings with your customer? Do you file the details in the appropriate place?			

Level 2 3.3   **Respond to the feelings expressed by the customer**

Performance criteria	Can do	Need more experience	Need training
(a) Do you accurately judge your customers' feelings by their behaviour, tone and by sensitively questioning them?			
(b) Do you adapt your own behaviour once you've acknowledge your customer's feelings?			
(c) Do you regularly check your customers' feelings to ensure you are dealing with them in the correct way?			
(d) Do you deal with customer complaints using the correct procedures?			

Level 2 3.4   **Adapt methods of communication to the customer**

Performance criteria	Can do	Need more experience	Need training
(a) Do you use the most appropriate form of communication face-to-face, in writing, by telephone, by body language, to keep customers informed about current and future services?			
(b) Do you use the most appropriate written and spoken language to suit your customer?			
(c) Do you chose the best method to communicate with customers who are disabled or have a language difference?			
(d) Do you regularly check that your customers understand what you're communicating to them?			
(e) Do you acknowledge when you have a communication difficulty? Do you seek help to resolve problems if you can't deal with them yourself?			

CASE STUDIES

Virginia keeps her cool

It is July and the activity centre is fully booked. A group from Germany have just arrived and Virginia Plain is preparing to greet them. What they forgot to inform her is that the leader has recently had an accident and is wheelchair-bound. The group's accommodation is on the second floor of a three-storey block and there is no wheelchair access.

She settles the group in, taking the leader to the staff room in the main building. She explains she will try to transfer his room to one on the ground floor in the same building.

She immediately checks the group list for visitors booked on the ground floor who arrived earlier. Checking their programme she can see they are on the canoe lake. She walks to the lake and locates their leader, explains the problem and asks if two of their group would be willing to move. Because she has a good relationship with the leader they agree to help out.

Lee emerges from the black cloud

Lee Henry is also on the lake. Today was supposed to be his day off but Bryan Houghton programmed him to take the canoe session. When he complained Bryan informed him if he didn't like it he could always get a job elsewhere.

Lee resentfully collects the group. The leader has met him before and can't understand the change in him. The last time they were there the group loved his jokey manner and enjoyed his company at dinner.

Half-way through the session, as Lee attempts to get the group to raft-up, one of the group accidentally knocks another with his paddle. The boy's temper suddenly flares and he tries to hit the offender, endangering all the canoeists. Lee immediately forgets his resentment at having to work. It isn't the group's fault and he really does like working with them.

He pacifies both boys and begins to joke with them, making them laugh so that the rest of the session is both enjoyable and fun.

Kelly helps a nervous customer

Kelly Chinn is giving change to a group of four girls when she notices a young boy enter Reception. He's looking at a notice board but doesn't appear to be interested in the information. She can see from his non-verbal signals he's nervous and appears to want something but is frightened to ask.

'Can I help you?' she asks when the girls have gone. She smiles warmly towards him to encourage him, asking him his name and which group he's with. As she continues to talk to him he begins to relax until he's ready to talk. He wants to go to his room but is embarrassed because he can't remember how to get there.

Kelly finds a map of the building from her filing system. She checks the Reception register and finds where the boy is located. Using a red pen, she draws a line from Reception to his room, continually checking that he understands. Finally, she tells him to come straight back to Reception if he can't find it and she'll take him there herself.

DISCUSSION POINTS

1. What are your personal strengths when dealing with customers?

2. What are your personal weaknesses when dealing with customers?

3. Can you remember an occasion when you or a colleague had to deal with an angry customer? What did you learn from the way you or they dealt with the situation?

4
Improving Your Customer Service

IMPROVING YOUR OWN PERFORMANCE

Skills for front-line staff

Most companies expect front-line staff dealing with customers to have the following skills:

- Good communication skills including the ability to talk clearly and have a good command of English, use the telephone properly and be able to write a letter using the correct grammar and spelling.

- Be able to get on with a wide range of people.

- Good social skills – know how to act from the time you greet a customer to the time you say goodbye. This should include the ability to listen.

- Be well groomed – not only by dressing smartly but by paying attention to cleanliness.

- Be able to organise yourself and your work.

- Have the ability to stay calm under pressure.

If you don't have these basic skills you can improve yourself – by reading training material and working on self-study courses, attending company-held courses, enrolling at night-school, watching others and learning from them.

Systems and procedures

Many companies put their new staff through an 'induction period' when they learn about laid-down guidelines on how to deal with an enquiry, how to handle customer complaints, the time within which staff are expected to answer telephone calls or reply to letters, etc. They may send existing staff on training courses to improve their standards.

All companies have 'systems and procedures' – what they expect staff to do and how to do it. Even if these 'systems and procedures' aren't written down, staff are still expected to follow the guidelines.

Example
Jo is new to Dice Services. She is shown by Shaun how to write down incoming phone calls in the telephone log. 'Can you also send the post out by 4 o'clock? And don't forget to write the details in that book,' he said, pointing to the outgoing mail book.

Finding out about your company's systems

Many companies are working towards/have achieved the ISO9002 Award (International Standards Office). The Award is granted when a company has met certain standards with its paperwork and systems. The details are usually kept in a file or portfolio. All staff should know how to use the file to check procedures.

If your company isn't working towards the ISO9002, find out exactly what is expected from you. If you can't find someone to make a comment, you may have to set your own standards for now.

Tips for setting standards

Telephone
The national standard for answering the telephone is to pick up the receiver before the fourth ring. You should say, 'good morning' or 'good afternoon' before introducing your company's name. That way the person calling has the chance to tune in to what you're saying and know they've got through to the right place. Smile when you answer – it will show in your voice. Keep a check on calls by filling in an incoming telephone log (see Figure 11).

Face-to-face
Acknowledge customers immediately if there are no others in the shop, or as soon as you've finished with the last customer (even if it's to say you won't be a moment while you complete some paperwork). If you work on a reception desk you could keep a visitors' register (see Figure 12).

Letters
Never leave a letter on your desk for days. It may get buried and lost forever. If you don't know how to deal with it ask someone to help or pass it on. Don't reply or take action if you aren't authorised to do so. Some companies use incoming and outgoing mail books – does yours? (See Figure 13.)

Exercise: your organisation's systems and procedures

Use your own knowledge of your company's systems to answer the following:

1. How long should you let the telephone ring before answering?

2. What do you say when you answer the telephone?

3. How long should you keep a caller on hold before returning to apologise:

   – if you can't locate the person they want to speak to?

   – if you're trying to find some information to help them?

4. If you take a message for someone who's unavailable where do you put the message:

   – on their desk? ☐

   – in a pigeon hole? ☐

   – on a notice board? ☐

   – write it in a book? ☐

   – other? ☐

5. When a customer enters the shop or office, how soon do you acknowledge them?

6. If you're busy with someone else do you:

   – speak to the new customer and apologise for delay? ☐

   – get someone else to help? ☐

   – ignore them? ☐

   – other? ☐

7. When letters are received do you:

   – pass them on to someone else for reply? ☐

   – rough out a reply and get someone else to check your grammar, spelling, etc? ☐

   – write the reply yourself with supervision? ☐

8. How soon do you reply to a letter received from a customer:

   – straightaway? ☐

   – the next day? ☐

   – by the end of the week? ☐

   – if you need to research information, acknowledge straightaway and reply as soon as you can? ☐

   – if you need to research information, reply as soon as you can? ☐

   – other? ☐

9. Do you consider the following three factors when you reply to a letter:

   – how fast a reply is required? ☐

   – which is the best method to send the reply (Royal Mail service, fax, telephone, e-mail)? ☐

   – how much each method will cost? ☐

10. Where do you file reply copies of letters:

   – on computer? ☐

   – filing tray? ☐

   – with customer's letter in their own file? ☐

   – you don't keep a copy? (naughty!) ☐

   – other? ☐

Date	Time	Caller	Taken by	Passed to
15.9.9-	9.15	IMOGEN BELL		LISSA R.
	9.30	SIMON DAWSON		JANE S.
	9.32	BECCA HOUGHTON		ZENA P.
	9.41	JEREMY DAVIES		LISSA R.
	10.05	ANDREW BATCHELOR		LISSA R.
	10.14	JASON SMITH		JANE S.

Fig. 11. Telephone log.

Date	Visitor's Name and company	To see	Arrival Time	Depart Time	Comments
22.9.9-	JASON SMITH	JANE S.	10.30	11.49	
	SIMON DAWSON	JANE S.	2.30	4.00	2nd interview 30.9.9-

Fig. 12. Visitors' register.

Date	From	Passed to	Content	Signature
28.8.9-	Universal Tools	Accounts	Chq £196.00	
	Dia Services	Accounts	Invoice	
	McCarthys	Sales	Order	
	Claires	Circulation Slip	Stationery Catalogue	
	HSE	"	Riddor 95 Regs	
29.8.9-	Wickham Park	Manager	Letter	
	Encon	Accounts	Chq £896.00	
	Solent Diamond	Sales	Letter	

Fig. 13. Incoming mail book.

LISTENING TO CUSTOMERS

The ten rules of listening

1. *Stop talking*: you have two ears and one tongue – that must tell you something.

2. *Get yourself ready to listen*: if you have time, prepare questions and comments beforehand. This will free your mind to listen.

3. *Help your talker to relax*: if they feel at ease they will feel more free to talk.

4. *Get rid of any distractions*: don't tap the desk, shuffle papers or doodle on a pad. Focus your mind on what the talker is saying.

5. *Be sympathetic*: try to see the point of view being expressed. Try to meet the talker half-way.

6. *Be patient*: if the speaker pauses it doesn't mean they've finished speaking. Even if it's a long pause, wait.

7. *Avoid personal prejudice*: if something in the person's manner irritates you or they say something that winds you up, don't allow it to distract you.

8. *Listen for changes in tone*: the volume and tone show a person's reaction to what you're saying.

9. *Be selective and listen for ideas*: listen for ideas, not just words. Isolated bits and pieces don't make up the whole meaning of the words.

10. *Watch for non-verbal signals*: remember Chapter 3 and look for those gestures, eye movements and expressions which give you important messages if you're talking to someone face-to-face.

Don't forget to ask questions
Find out what the customer wants by listening but don't forget to ask questions when you aren't clear on any point. Don't be blunt or pushy, but speak clearly, watching for any non-verbal signals. If they are nervous and feel as though they are on trial they may clam up and make your job that much harder.

Avoiding negative signs
Be careful not to show negative signs:

• smirking if customers don't understand something you've told them

CUSTOMER FEEDBACK

We endeavour to give our customers the best service possible. To ensure our standards are maintained we would appreciate your comments. Would you kindly complete the details below and return the form to the address overleaf.   Thank you.

Service used:... *Kitchen fitment* ....

Was the job completed to your satisfaction?: Yes/No̶

If no, please give details below:.......................................

Skirting board not finished propely ....

....

How would you rate the service you received?

Excellent ☐ Good ☐ Fair ☑ Poor ☐ Unacceptable ☐

How would you rate the quality of the fitments?

Excellent ☐ Good ☐ Fair ☐ Poor ☐ Unacceptable ☑

Additional comments:

....

....

Fig. 14. Example feedback form.

- impatience if they can't make up their mind quickly

- amusement at their expense if they say something you feel has nothing to do with the purpose of their visit.

Got it!
Check regularly to make sure you're offering them the sort of information, product or service they're after. You may have got the wrong idea and the customer is too embarrassed to tell you unless you ask.

USING FEEDBACK

Immediate feedback
We like to know if we're doing something right or wrong. Customer feedback is often immediate and tells us whether:

- the customer's happy with the product or service

- they're not satisfied.

You may not openly acknowledge the customer is happy or dissatisfied and they may not tell you outright, but most people get a gut reaction about such things.

Asking for feedback
If people don't comment on a product or service, ask their opinion. Constantly try to find out what they think about the quality of the goods you sell and reliability of the services you offer.

If you have feedback forms (see Figure 14), issue them. If it's your company's policy to get customers to write in your visitors' book, point it out to them. Tell them you welcome any comments they may wish to make. Regularly pass on the comments you receive to the correct authority who can make any changes if they are necessary.

If you've personally received feedback and feel you can do something to improve the reliability of the service you give, mention it to your manager or use your initiative – as long as it's within your area of authority.

Working with others
When you're trying to improve the service you give to customers, you should talk to your colleagues and managers about the way you deliver goods or services. Is there a better way to do it?

Let other people know if you have made improvements in your own area of responsibility because of an extra effort on your part:

- Have you picked up comments from customers? Could you learn something from them?

- If people have passed on tips and hints, have you taken notice of them?

- Have you tried new ways to improve service delivery and reliability?

ACTING QUICKLY

Supplying goods and services quickly

Whatever the customer wants you should be able to supply it or offer a similar product or service. You should know where to get further supplies/information if they aren't immediately available. Each time you apologise and explain something is out of stock you risk losing a potential customer.

Remember to:

- Find out what the customer really wants, whether they ask directly or you have to question them about the service they require.

- Make an extra effort to avoid delays in getting what the customer needs.

- Be flexible when you help them – with proper authorisation you may be able to bend the rules slightly.

- Ask your supervisor/manager/others for practical help to supply the service needs of your customer.

Brochures, handouts and advertising bumph

Advertising literature and information is often produced outside the company. It is aimed to show how professional and reliable the company is. The effort costs a lot of money each year.

What a waste it would be if you, the person dealing with the customer, forgot to get a new supply of brochures and had nothing to hand to an interested customer when they made an enquiry.

Keep a check on your stock and if you take the last batch tell someone in authority. It's no good leaving it to someone else to notice.

Equipment

Ensure the equipment you use is in good working order. How can you serve a customer quickly if your till has broken down or you can't open it to get at your supply of change? If the fax is broken how can you send information immediately?

Forms

It is important to keep a good stock of blank forms. When a customer wants to join your club, apply for credit, become a member of your building society, if you've run out of the correct forms they may not come back.

Example
Simon was bored. It was a wet day; he had nothing to do. He went to a local shop to join the video club to hire a video. He took with him his cheque book, bank card and birth certificate to prove his identity. However, he was shocked and angry when the shop assistant said he'd have to come back the next day.

'Sorry,' she said, turning her back on him to serve another customer, 'we're out of forms. You'll have to come back tomorrow when my supervisor's in.'

Simon joined a club in the next village and vowed never to use the first shop again.

Stocktaking

Make sure you have a full stock of the items you sell. You should regularly check your shelves and re-stock those items which are running low. You should also keep a close eye on stored stock:

- Have you just emptied a packing case of the last of a line?

- Can you see there are only two boxes of a popular item left?

- Do you have a stock order list?

- Do you regularly place items on it which you know you're short of?

- Do you check expiry dates to make sure your stock isn't past its shelf-life?

If you do run out of stock, apologise. Offer to order it for the customer immediately or suggest another similar product. If they require an emergency service and your fitters are busy, consider whether the emergency warrants urgent action, e.g. taking the fitter off another job.

Item	No. in stock	In good order
Literature including brochures on services, products, courses, special offers, etc.		
Stationery including envelopes, headed paper, photocopy paper, fax roll		
Forms including application forms, registration cards, legal contracts, etc.		
Small stores including computer disks, batteries, etc.		
Mechanical or electronic including calculators, scales, computers, credit card machines, etc.		
Consumables including pens, pencils, Tippex, printer cartridges and ribbons, etc.		

Fig. 15. Stationery check.

Stationery check
As controlling stock of all items includes stationery, check your own cupboard for the items listed in Figure 15.

Showing your customers your best side
Having all the equipment and supplies ready and available will help to present a positive image to the customer. But it's all wasted if your own behaviour is appalling.

• You must always treat your customers with consideration and care. Even when you're under stress you should help them as much as possible.

• Remember the way you come across to a customer and how to handle them reflects on your company. Always keep up a high standard and act professionally even when you don't feel well or would rather be anywhere else but work.

• The equipment and supplies you use or deal with are your responsibility – you should either check them yourself or report to another person if there's a problem.

• Continually look for ways to improve your working relationships, not only with your customers but also with your colleagues. It's no good being polite to your customers and awful to the people you work with.

• Always act in a responsible way. Having a laugh and chatting to your colleagues may be a pleasant distraction from work if there are no customers around, but as soon as one appears you should stop immediately.

GETTING HELP WHEN NEEDED

Balancing act
Don't be frightened to go to someone else for help or advice when you're trying to perform a difficult balancing act – trying to please the customer while avoiding giving away your company's profits.

Unless you own the company there are always limits to what you are authorised to do. You should know these limits and if you don't, find out. Someone might be in a position to give an additional discount for cash or agree to fit an extra electrical socket free of charge. Are you in that position?

The best way to balance the company and customer's needs is to remember the following:

- Look at every option open to help give the customer what they want. If you can't come up with an answer yourself, you may have to talk to a colleague or go to people outside your organisation for help.

- Once you and the customer have identified how you can help then – whether it's an informal agreement, e.g. agreeing to delay a job until the customer returns from holiday the following day, or a formal agreement, e.g. a contract has been signed – you should check the customer understands what you've agreed. You should also inform any staff who may be affected.

- The agreement shouldn't cost the company money or increase the fee to the customer so much that they have a heart attack or take their business elsewhere.

- If there are limits to which your company will go regarding cost, time and resources, you should carefully explain these to the customer. You should be careful not to frighten the customer into thinking that you're only interested in the profit you'll make from them.

- Whatever you do, whether you've foreseen a problem might occur and have taken the initiative to sort it out, or you've been asked by a customer to deal with something, you must perform a balancing act to please both them and your company.

- Once you've gone over all the options and know you have solved the problem, check with your supervisor or manager to get their authority to continue.

- Remember to record the details somewhere – a memo, a short note, a report or an entry in the database or file. If the people you work with have to deal with the customer later, tell them what has happened. Pass them a copy of your report or memo to make sure they know what you've done so far.

COLLECTING EVIDENCE FOR YOUR NVQ

Listed below are a few examples of evidence you can collect for the following NVQ Elements:

Customer Service Level 2   **Level 3**
Element: 5.1 5.2 5.3   **Element: 3.1 3.2 3.3**

- Examples of brochures and information leaflets on your product/ service.

- Your company's Health and Safety at Work procedures.

- Stock lists.

- Orders for goods and services.

- Copies of literature and forms.

- Memos suggesting improvements to your system.

- Company policy on your organisation's limitations.

- Letters from customers thanking you for your help.

- A case study (see Chapter 9).

- Witness statements from colleagues/customers.

CHECKLIST

Level 2 5.1   **Respond promptly to the service needs of the customer**

Performance criteria	Yes	Need more experience	Need training
(a) Can you promptly and clearly identify what your customer's needs are?			
(b) Do you make extra unprompted efforts to avoid delaying your customers?			
(c) Do you make sure to be flexible when you use your company's current procedures so that you respond to what you customer needs?			
(d) Do you ask for practical help from your colleagues to make sure you deliver your customer's service needs?			

Level 2 5.2   **Use customer feedback
                                                   to improve service
                                                   reliability**

Performance criteria	Yes	Need more experience	Need training
(a) Do you consistently seek comments from customers about how reliable your service is?			
(b) Do you actively use customer feedback and pass comments back to the appropriate person or authority?			
(c) Do you try to improve the reliability of your service to customers as a result of their feedback?			
(d) Do you inform colleagues of improvements made based on feedback from customers?			

Level 2 5.3   **Work with others to
                                                   improve service reliability**

Performance criteria	Yes	Need more experience	Need training
(a) Do you use the ideas and experiences of colleagues to improve your own performance?			
(b) Do you let others know of improvements you've made within your own area of responsibility?			
(c) Do you regularly check with colleagues the current organisation procedures for service delivery?			
(d) Do you take action to let other people know of changes needed to improve service reliability?			
(e) When you've worked with others, do you use the outcomes to improve the service you offer?			

Level 3 3.1   **Respond to the needs and feelings expressed by the customer**

Performance criteria	Yes	Need more experience	Need training
(a) Can you find out what your customers need quickly, clearly and sensitively?			
(b) Are you able to gauge customers' feelings accurately by observing their behaviour and tone? Are you able to sensitively question them to clarify things?			
(c) Do you sensitively question customers to find out their needs?			
(d) Do you always adapt your own behaviour when you understand your customers' needs and feelings?			
(e) Do you regularly check your customers' needs and feelings and find out whether or not you are helping them?			

Level 3 3.2   **Present positive personal image to customer**

Performance criteria	Yes	Need more experience	Need training
(a) Do you always treat your customers courteously and helpfully, especially when you are under stress?			
(b) Do you maintain a high standard of appearance and behaviour when at work?			
(c) Do you make sure your equipment and supplies are available, up-to-date and in good working order?			
(d) Do you actively look for ways to improve your working relationships with customers and advise them of ways to perfect their health and safety?			
(e) Do you always make sure your own behaviour gives a good impression of your company to the customer?			

Level 3 3.3   **Balance the needs of customers and organisation**

Performance criteria	Yes	Need more experience	Need training
(a) Do you make a real effort to meet your customers' needs regardless of the problem?			
(b) Do you identify all the options available to bring mutual gain to all parties? Do you make sure they are clearly informed?			
(c) Do you make sure the formal or informal options are cost-effective for both parties?			
(d) Do you explain clearly and positively to the customer any limits to which your organisation works?			
(e) Do you take all possible actions to make sure conflict between customer needs and organisation limits are minimal?			
(f) Do you explore the flexible limits your organisation has to solve the problem? Do you confirm your proposed solution with others?			
(g) Do you clearly record, store and relay the outcomes of your proposal to any personnel who will be affected?			

CASE STUDIES

Lee helps a nervous customer

Lee is about to take a group of canoeists onto the lake. One of the girls looks particularly apprehensive. He asks the other instructor to carry on with the group while he takes the girl to one side. He helps her to relax by joking with her. Eventually, she tells him she can't swim and is frightened of water.

He reassures her she will be quite safe, explaining the purpose of the life jacket, and goes through the safety procedures. He promises he will stay next to her throughout the hour-long session. She finally agrees to have a go. Lee never strays far away and by the end of the hour she has completely forgotten about her fears.

Virginia runs out of headed notepaper

Virginia has been asked by the manager to talk to a group of headteachers who are planning to visit the Centre next year. While she is out of her office Bryan Houghton realises he has run out of the Centre's headed notepaper. He wants to send out a run of two hundred letters to mail-shot all schools in the south of England. He takes her supply but doesn't bother to tell her.

The following day the manager calls Virginia to his office and dictates several urgent letters to confirm the headteachers' bookings. He tells her they must go out that day. When she discovers she has no headed notepaper she is bewildered. She has some on order but isn't expecting it to arrive for at least two days.

She discovers who has taken it but it's too late to get the paper back. Bryan has already photocopied his letter onto all the sheets. She manages to find two stray sheets and asks the manager which are the most important letters, explaining her problem. She then telephones the print company and asks if they could make her order a priority so she can pick it up the following day.

Kelly uses her initiative

A young customer asks Kelly if he can use the telephone to call his mum to let her know he's arrived safely. If the visitor lived locally she would normally ask Virginia if it would be OK. As the boy is one of the German group she knows the call would be quite expensive. She decides she will have to turn down his request and explains that, unfortunately, she isn't able to allow him to telephone Germany unless he can pay for the call.

DISCUSSION POINTS

1. Can you deal with a customer complaint without it causing you too much stress? Who would you go to if the situation deteriorated and you knew you couldn't help the customer any further?

2. How often do you check your own equipment for safety? When was the last time you cleaned your computer, till, scales, cutting machine, etc.?

3. What are the limitations of your authority? Are you authorised to give discounts, extend your customers' credit limits or order new stock items you've never previously bought before?

5
Your Company's Good Reputation

WORKING WITH OTHER STAFF

Your behaviour affects others

Falling out with someone at work makes you feel miserable and wish you worked (or they worked) somewhere else. The effects show in the way you walk, talk and look. Often you keep your mouth shut and bite your tongue if the argument's with a senior member of staff, while you may have a bitter argument it it's a colleague.

Whoever the argument is with it will probably be noticed by the customers – especially if you act really unprofessionally and have a moan to them.

> *Example*
> A regular customer comes into the shop and asks why you've got such a long face. 'My manager's a real pig. He thinks he knows it all – telling me I've got to tidy up the counter display! Just because it's a bit of mess doesn't mean he's got to have a go at me.'

Others' reaction to your behaviour

How you deal with the situation will affect other people's behaviour towards you. If they are senior to you they have a right to correct you or give you advice on how to do a job. They may not do it in the manner you feel you deserve but you should be adult enough to accept a bit of criticism. If you sulk and moan they will think you're immature and childish.

If you've upset people at work it may also have an effect on what they are and aren't willing to do for you.

Many people develop a good working relationship with colleagues and outside contacts over a number of months or even years. But it doesn't last five minutes if a harsh word or thoughtless comment is spoken. That brief snide remark can undo all the goodwill you've cultivated for so long.

Remember the importance of developing constructive relationships:

- Recognise what it is you both need from each other.
- Work productively together.
- Help each other and give support when things get difficult.

Job description
You should have a job description which will show what your job responsibilities are. An organisation chart will clarify where you stand in the staff line-up. Once you know where you fit into the company you are in a better position to take orders from or give instructions to the people you work with.

Having authority over someone doesn't mean continually bossing them about. It means you use them to their full potential in the most positive way. You are responsible not only for what they do but for how they do it. Their work output is down to your supervision and the quality for you to check.

How do you maintain positive work relationships with your colleagues?

1. If you see your manager, supervisor or a work colleague is under pressure when they're dealing with a customer, do you offer them practical help? For instance, if they are trying to sort out a problem and need copies of information, do you offer to photocopy it for them? If they can't find the right size garment do you offer to check the stock room?

2. Remember to continually update your knowledge about products or services and show an interest in all you do. Ask the people you work with for information and watch how they do things. Increase your knowledge about your company's goods and services by asking questions. Write to suppliers and ask for more information and details of new products.

3. Improve your working relationships by taking opportunities to help others and prove you are a good, reliable worker. Pass on things you've learnt to your colleagues. If you have some technical knowledge about a product or service, share this with others. But be warned: don't be a know-it-all – that can be more irritating than not passing on information at all.

4. Offer to help out if you see someone is stretched or is having difficulty finishing a job or dealing with a customer. If you're asked to do something, do it willingly especially if it is going to improve the service you offer to customers.

SORTING OUT PERSONAL DIFFERENCES

Working under supervision

When you work closely with others you're bound to have personal differences. But people can't read your mind. If you feel you've been unjustifiably accused of something you know you haven't done, you should try to sort it out. If you know you've been unreasonable, you should be mature enough to admit it.

It's always hard to face up to a problem and if you feel you can't do it yourself you could always ask a third party, perhaps a supervisor, for their opinion and/or advice on what to do.

If you aren't able to sort things out, it may affect your work and consequently your efficiency in dealing with customers.

Problems arise for different reasons:

- You've promised to get a job done but haven't been able to meet the deadline. You haven't told anyone because you're worried you have let them down.

- You've been asked to find some information and haven't been able to locate it. The person who wants it is annoyed because they've been waiting an hour.

- You've been asked to do a job but don't know how to do it. You're too embarrassed to tell anyone.

- Something happens, e.g. a machine breaks down or an unexpected visitor arrives and interrupts you, and you can't concentrate on the job in hand. Things start to go wrong and the more you try to carry on the worse the problem gets.

- Someone gives you advice or information on how to do the job. Before you've started, someone gives you different advice or information.

- You are in the middle of a job and a colleague makes unreasonable demands on your time. You're trying to please everyone, but please no one in the end.

- People are unreasonable or unfair and you feel resentful because you believe you don't deserve such harsh treatment.

- People withhold the information you need to do your job properly. You have asked them several times but they seem to enjoy being awkward.

- Some people are naturally grumpy and difficult. They seem to enjoy winding you up.

Problem-solving exercise

It may help to try this simple exercise to find answers to problems yourself.

List all the things you've identified as a problem. Also list the reasons you think they happened and what you can do about them now or next time they happen. Look at the examples in the chart below.

Examples of problem-solving	
What is happening?	*Why it's happening and what I can do about it?*
Tried to finish urgent letters in time to catch the post. Missed post.	Constantly interrupted by people asking me to do photocopying. I will have to explain about the urgent letters next time and if the photocopying is urgent they'll have to do it themselves. I'll do it tomorrow if they're prepared to wait.
Took me ages to work out how to use the new till.	Didn't ask the supervisor how to use the till before she left the shop. Make sure I ask any questions about using new equipment when my supervisor is around.
People expecting me to do jobs that aren't my responsibility – it's making me fall behind in my own work.	I want to impress people – show them I can do anything that's asked of me. I should admit I don't have the time.
Each time I ask Carina for some stock she says she can't issue it unless I have written approval.	I upset her by taking an item without booking it out. Now she's making my life difficult. I should apologise and hope I can rebuild a good working relationship.

Some problems are out of your hands, and there is very little you can do about them, but always try to be positive about every situation. In a perfect world, talking about problems is the first step to solving them. Unfortunately, it isn't always that simple. If you know what the problem is, however, you are half-way there.

Working in a supervisory position

If you are in a supervisory position, you may have a different type of problem to sort out. There are several ways to reduce conflicts even if you can't completely resolve them. Look at the examples in the chart below.

Examples of problem-solving – supervisors

What is happening?	Why it's happening and what I can do about it?
One of the staff isn't doing their job properly.	They've lost interest because another person was promoted ahead of them. Talk to them and discuss where they feel their strengths lie and what their job aspirations are.
Two of my staff don't seem to do as much as they should and I'm stuck with all the work.	Perhaps they haven't got enough to challenge them. Give them more responsibility. I may have to give them extra time and training to make sure they understand what I want.
I'm changing Lissa's job role. Last time I made a change we fell out for a few weeks.	I didn't talk to her about the change last time. This time I'll arrange a meeting and see how she feels first.
Crystal wants to work on Reception but I've said no because she doesn't know how to use the switchboard or answer the phone properly.	If she's keen think of ways to help her. Arrange for training beforehand. If she does well arrange for a trial run on Reception.

How to get more help

There are many other publications which are specifically geared towards managing people, dealing with stress and coping with situations which seem almost impossible to sort out. (See the Further Reading section at the end of this book.)

WORKING AS A TEAM

Team-building

Building a strong work team is the basis for good business. In a team each person is given some responsibility which ultimately motivates them to do better. If you are in a position to lead and guide (even if it's only by example) there are three things you should know about managing people:

- how to handle conflict
- how to motivate other staff
- how to build a successful team.

Motivating others

How to motivate others is a skill. It can be learnt and improved on. The following guidelines could help you make a start.

- Get to know staff as individuals
  - What are their interests?
  - What pleases them?
  - What makes them angry?

- What are their strengths? Help them to build on these.

- What are their weaknesses? Help them to disguise theirs.

- Don't give them the jobs you don't want or can't be bothered to do. Delegate work they'll find interesting.

- Help them to solve their own problems.

- Don't rule by threat or fear. Don't put out false rumours to worry them.

- Encourage and support people who have problems. If they're finding their job difficult, give help or advice on how to do it more efficiently.

- Give praise and encouragement if they do a job well, no matter how small the job or task is.

- If they are under attack or being unfairly judged, stick up for them and protect them if you can.

- If you have a company scheme which recognises performance, make sure staff who have achieved something get the credit.

- Be open to staff ideas and encourage them to share them with you. They may have thought of something you hadn't or be able to do something better than you.

- Interest them by giving them challenges but don't stretch them too far or overload them so that they fail.

- If you are to make a decision involve them if you can.

- Always keep them up-to-date with anything which may affect them.

Assumptions
We all think our view of things is the way others are seeing situations. Quite often we're wrong:

> 'Man's behaviour can be observed, measured and explained. However, his mind is not open to inspection.'

ANTICIPATING BUSY PERIODS

Time management
Every business has busy periods, times when you know you and the other staff are going to be pushed to the limits. For instance:

- first day of the January sales
- end of the month accounts
- Friday shoppers
- bank holiday guests
- Friday afternoon when the boss is clearing his desk and decides to dictate several letters.

You must learn to value your time. It's your most precious resource and the only one you can never replace. You won't be able to stop all the time-wasting things you do overnight but make a start by:

- being aware of what you're doing that wastes time

- beginning to change your working habits.

Action Plan for supplying room and equipment for conference on 14 November 199X:

Task	Date for completion	Action by	Tick when done
Book overhead projector	end Sept	SP	✓
Arrange for screen to be fixed to wall	beg. Nov	BF	✓
Bring chairs up from cellar	12 Nov	KH	
Clean room and put chairs and projector in place	12 Nov	KH	
Contact customer for last minute arrangements	end Oct	SP	✓
Organise staff to supply tea and coffee	end Oct	SP	✓
Check number of cups, saucers and spoons	end Oct	SP	✓
Buy tea, coffee, milk, sugar, biscuits	13 Nov	KH	

Fig. 16. Action plan.

There are certain job roles which can't be controlled by managing your time – if you are an administrator or a personal assistant your boss may make so many demands on your time you can't change it.

Planning

Planning will help you make a start on managing your time more efficiently.

- If you planned badly yesterday it not only wastes time but can also lead to a crisis.
- Crises cause problems which have to be resolved.
- Problems take time to solve.
- Bad planning can disrupt work for days ahead.

Making plans

Many people manage their time by working to action plans or schedules or by filling in a diary with events planned or tasks they know they have to do. Some people make a rough list as a memory jogger and cross out the entries once the job has been done. Examples of an **action plan** and a **staff review schedule** are given in Figures 16 and 17.

The sort of things you can put in your **diary** include:

- jobs listed on your action plan
- jobs carried forward to a future date
- jobs which have to be done by a particular date
- jobs which aren't confirmed – use a pencil for these until they're definite
- events which happen regularly
- important events you mustn't forget
- timed appointments and visits.

Electronic organisers

There are a variety of small purse-sized organisers on the market. They can include a diary with an alarm to remind you of important dates; database for names, addresses, telephone numbers, etc.; clock (with alarm); wordprocessor with spell-checker; spreadsheet for your accounts.

Security of your equipment is important so remember not to leave

	Jan	Feb	Mar	Apr	May	Jun	Jul	Aug	Sep	Oct	Nov	Dev
Rosemary			X									
Jackie									X			
Justin					X							
David					X							
Ray											X	
Joshua						X						

Fig. 17. Staff review schedule.

it on your desk. Not only will you lose an expensive piece of office equipment but because they hold so much information you may feel your life has ended as well!

Helping yourself and others
Whichever method you use to organise yourself it's important to remember why you're doing it.

It isn't to give yourself more time to play games on the computer or to read your favourite magazine. It's to organise your work so you can anticipate your customers' needs and help them to the best of your ability.

'No man is an island'
You can't do it all on your own unless you're your own boss and there is no one else. Even in this situation you would probably enlist help from elsewhere if things got too busy. If you're a member of a team you're there to help each other.

- Ask for help and advice from your managers or others in your company when you know you've reached your limits. These limits may be your own competence to do something or company limits where you have reached the boundaries of your authority.

- If your workload becomes so heavy you can't maintain a reliable service to your customers, assertively ask for practical help.

- Offer practical help to your colleagues if you see their workload has become heavy during a particularly busy period.

- Make that extra effort to avoid delays in providing service to your customers even if it means you have to put aside a less important job you'd planned to do.

- If there is a particularly busy period or an unexpectedly heavy workload to finish, make a positive effort. Don't moan and complain but willingly make that extra effort even if it means working an extra five minutes into your lunch break (as long as it doesn't happen all the time).

- Use previous experience and knowledge of your business to plan for future heavy workloads. Anticipate when these peaks will occur and plan your work around them.

- Don't force your own ideas and experience onto your workmates – consider their feelings and get their co-operation without bullying them. Be sensitive and discuss things with them to ensure the customers' needs are met by a well-motivated team of people who work with each other and not against each other.

What's in it for me?

It's not wrong to think about what's in it for you when you do someone else a favour to help them out. Don't think of them in money terms but as building up favours which can be called on later when you need some help.

Assertiveness

Being assertive doesn't mean being bossy – it means being up-front with a request.

- If you need help or assistance, you're quite entitled to ask for it.

- If you genuinely don't have time to do something, you are at liberty to say so.

- If you feel it inappropriate to take on a task, you can turn down the request.

How you do this will have an impact on the people you're dealing with. You can upset or annoy them if you do it the wrong way.

- Be direct and don't keep apologising because you feel guilty for asking/turning down a request.

- You don't have to justify yourself but you should give a reason for your request or refusal.

- Don't lie.

- Don't flatter someone just to get your own way. You shouldn't have to bribe staff to co-operate or creep to get out of a job.

- Have clear in your mind what you want to achieve as there will probably be a debate between you and the other person. If they are refusing to help you, they may have a justifiable reason – listen to them.

- If you really are unable to help, suggest other ways you can assist.

COLLECTING EVIDENCE FOR YOUR NVQ

Listed below are a few examples of evidence you can collect for the following NVQ Elements:

Customer Service Level 2   **Level 3**
Element: 1.3   **Element: 1.2   1.3**

- Your job description.

- A case study (see Chapter 9).

- An organisation chart.

- Copies of work schedules, diaries and action plans.

- A flow chart to show the channels you need to go through to resolve a problem when things go wrong.

- Minutes of meetings where you have made a suggestion for increasing motivation, rearranging job roles, etc.

- Witness statements from colleagues/customers.

CHECKLIST

Level 2 1.3   **Maintain positive working relationships with colleagues**

Performance criteria	Yes	Need more experience	Need training
(a) Do you offer practical help to colleagues when they're under pressure in order to deliver a good service to your customers?			
(b) Do you continually update your own knowledge of your products or services by working positively with colleagues – share information, pass on tips, etc.			
(c) Do you continually try to improve relationships with your colleagues by making an extra effort?			
(d) Do you share your own knowledge and experience of your company's service systems with other members of staff?			
(e) Do you co-operate with the others members of staff to make sure you give your customers the best possible service?			

Level 3 1.2   **Organise own work pattern to respond to the needs of the customer**

Performance criteria	Yes	Need more experience	Need training
(a) Do you ask your colleagues for help when you know you're out of your depth, whether it's when you've reached the limits of your own authority or when you really don't know how to answer a customer query or enquiry?			
(b) Do you get practical help assertively to make sure you maintain a good customer service during peaks in your workload?			
(c) Do you offer practical help to colleagues when you know they're having a busy peak in their workload?			
(d) Can you avoid delays in customer service through your own unprompted extra efforts?			
(e) Do you make positive responses to meet abnormal and unexpected workloads?			
(f) Do you use your previous experience to make plans to meet the known demands of future workloads?			
(g) Can you respond sensitively to your team and customer needs using your own ideas and previous experiences?			

Performance criteria	Yes	Need more experience	Need training
(a) Do you continually try to find opportunities to improve working relationships with your colleagues?			
(b) Do you talk to other staff about the organisational procedures you use for monitoring customer service? Do you discuss whether they could be improved?			
(c) Do you make it your business to keep in contact with external suppliers and regulatory bodies to keep the information you hold up-to-date?			
(d) Do you scan information in magazines or suppliers' pamphlets? If you hear of a new contact, product or service which is likely to benefit your customers do you find out more?			
(e) Do you work with the other staff to provide your customers with a reliable service?			

CASE STUDIES

Kelly gets promotion

Virginia has decided to give more responsibility to Kelly. She has proved she can cope well with the job she has been given and is showing a flair for dealing with figures. The part-time Accounts Clerk is to retire next year and Virginia suggests Kelly may be interested in working alongside the Clerk to learn about accounts with a view to taking over next year when Kelly is to be fully employed by the Centre.

Kelly says she enjoys working on Reception and wouldn't like to give it up. She's also concerned she might not be able to cope with the additional work.

Virginia suggests Kelly is given an assistant – a trainee whom she can train herself. She suggests Kelly should continue to work on Reception in a supervisory capacity. They agree to a three-months trial after which they will have another meeting to discuss how things are progressing before a formal agreement is met.

Lee's day off

Bryan has informed Lee that he will have to drive a group to their horse-riding session at Wickham as he doesn't have another driver. Although Bryan knew about this two days ago he has only just informed Lee. He is aware it is Lee's day off but work is his priority and believes it should be Lee's as well.

Lee had planned to go out with Carina. Although he's complained, he knows he has no choice but to drive the group. He argues with Carina who tells him he should stick up for himself. He is angry and sullen and doesn't speak to the group all the way to Wickham.

Virginia sets her electronic organiser

Virginia is in the middle of an important meeting with the Head of the Centre and the Board of Directors. She has recently purchased an electronic organiser and is making full use of it. She continually carries it in her bag.

Two weeks ago she set an alarm and when it sounds she doesn't realise it's her organiser. As the sound continues to disrupt the meeting the Directors search the room for its source. Virginia is embarrassed when she realises it's coming from her bag.

DISCUSSION POINTS

1. Have you been involved in conflict at work? What happened? What did you do about it? Would you deal with it differently if a similar thing happened again?

2. What motivates you to do something – interest, personal gain, a desire to please?

3. Do you work as part of a team? Who leads the team and what do you admire (if anything) about the way they do it?

6
Keeping Yourself Up-to-date

UPDATING YOUR OWN INFORMATION

How to keep up-to-date

No one can force you to read the company minutes or reports or insist you look at suppliers' magazines, catalogues and information sheets. But if you don't, you will be ignorant of changes and at a disadvantage compared with other staff who make the effort.

Remember to:

1. Read staff memos, company magazines, newsletters and literature, etc.

2. Have an enquiring mind and if you see something new, ask your supervisor about it.

3. Listen to more senior staff when they discuss a new product or service.

4. Study customers' legal rights and new legislation, which are sometimes the topic of newspaper articles and television news programmes. Don't ignore them as boring.

5. Attend meetings and supplier events – collect information and listen to what's being said.

Circulation slip

(See Figure 18.) This is a very simple form which is attached to the front of the magazine/document. On it are listed the people who should see it and a space for a signature once it's been read. It is then passed on to the next person on the list, and so on.

Problems with the system

Its fault lies with people who don't read information immediately but put it in their filing tray or drawer and forget it's there. This means other staff lose out on up-to-date information.

```
CIRCULATION SLIP

Description of item:  ...........................

Name                          Date      Date
                              Received  Passed on

Dee Pink

Crystal McCarthy

Val Green

Terry Powell

Brian Pease

Pat Head

Ken Dimmer

Dee Thorn

Andy Dijken          23/7/9 - Andy Dixon

Vanessa Courage

Sue Batten

Angela Richards

Jean Naumczeck




To be returned to the Resources Room
```

Fig. 18. Circulation slip.

To combat this hiccup give priority to certain names on the circulation slip, i.e. those people you know will read and act on new information. Most employers soon learn which members of staff are innovative and forward looking. Try to make yourself one of them.

Photocopying

Photocopying should be used if all the staff need a copy of the information, for instance, the latest update from the Health and Safety Executive, Trade Descriptions, etc.

Passing it on

Of course, it's no good finding out all this updated information if you're going to keep it to yourself. Don't feel embarrassed or afraid to mention it, even if it turns out there's a memo or report on its way with the same details.

Protecting confidentiality

Not all the information you find out should be passed on to your customers. Some things are confidential to a company, e.g. a supplier is offering you a particularly large discount on certain items.

You should also remember the Copyright laws and Data Protection Act (see Chapter 2).

Having a regular routine

Make it part of your routine to scan or examine any documents which come your way. The information may come from inside or outside your organisation and may be in the form of minutes or reports, regular magazines or newsletters. It may also come from another source such as a government directive (new rules made in Parliament) or from a customer or supplier.

When you're passing on information to customers make sure you don't confuse them with too much jargon.

Example
Denise has just read an article about the latest photographic fluids which cut developing time down by half. She feels quite enthusiastic about them and is dying to pass on the information to the next customer in the shop.

Unfortunately, the next customer has only just embarked on photography as a hobby. As Denise discusses the virtues of different fluids the customer feels totally lost. Finally she interrupts.

'I'm sorry, but I don't understand what you're talking about. I only came in for a black and white film!'

Discovering what the customer wants

If a customer asks you for information, make sure the details you give are what they want whether it's about:

- a product or service they've particularly asked for; or
- a product or service they want advice about.

Give accurate and relevant advice or information as quickly and fully as possible. Inform in a way which will avoid or lessen any worry. For instance, if it's about changes in the building regulations and they are currently having an extension built, explain how it will affect them and how you will help them overcome any problems.

Filing new information

Any information you receive should be filed in the right place so that it can be found again at a moment's notice. If you have to open up another file or are going to place it in a certain place, let the other staff know where you've put it. They might need to find it when you're not around.

KEEPING THE CUSTOMER INFORMED

Methods of communication

There are several ways to keep the customer informed:

Face-to-face
When they visit in person to buy or order goods and services, pay a bill, make a complaint, ask for information, bring goods back and request a refund, etc.

In writing
If a customer has requested information by telephone or post, or cannot wait in the shop or office for the details they want. It may also be a written confirmation to back up a telephone or verbal conversation.

Fax or telephone
Urgent information could be faxed or telephoned. If it is faxed and the information is confidential, warn the person receiving it that it's

on its way – they can then be there to receive it without the rest of the office seeing.

Computers
The Internet is the most rapidly growing method of getting/sending information. You can contact a user in most countries and have an immediate two-way computer conversation.

To get up-and-running you need a suitable computer and be connected to a service provider such as CompuServe or CIX. They charge an initial registration fee and monthly hire charges for the line. On top of this there is a charge for the time spent linked to their computer via the telephone line.

See a specialist for more information.

Which method?
The method you use depends on the situation and might also depend on cost.

Example
Andy Dijken has to get an urgent estimate to the local council for a meeting the next day. He is hoping to win the contract for refurbishing forty council houses and his estimate is to be discussed along with two others.

To be absolutely certain the estimate arrives safely, Andy decides he will have to deliver it himself. It means missing a staff meeting and travelling across town in the rush hour – but the profit he will make if he gets the contract makes the loss of time worthwhile.

Methods of selling yourself to your customers

Mail shot
A mail shot is a letter sent to people you would like to be your customers. You may not have previously been in contact with them but feel you can offer them something.

You probably get mail shots all the time yourself, but you would know them by their modern name – 'junk mail'! Call them what you like, there are many people who do buy the offers they receive news of in the post.

Circular letter
Circular letters circulate information to new and existing customers – about a new product, a special offer, a change in your company's way

of doing things, etc. It is a standard letter and is designed to pass on the same information to all customers.

Example
Tom has just bought new premises from which to operate his nursery business. The easiest way to make sure all customers are aware of the new address, telephone number and new lines on offer is to send a circular letter.

Local newspaper advertising
It might be appropriate to advertise a special offer in the local newspaper. Even better, if the offer is something out of the ordinary, why not contact the news desk to see if the paper will do an article on you, the product or your business? Find the number in the telephone directory or look at the local paper.

- Does a particular journalist specialise in articles about businesses?

- Does the newspaper run regular features on new businesses or special business events?

Ring the offices and ask for the appropriate person by name. Or, if you're still not sure, just ring and explain why you're calling. Newspapers get calls each and every day about similar things – that's how they get their stories.

Open day
Existing and prospective customers are invited to view your goods or see examples of work you've carried out. Usually you will have to supply refreshments or offer another incentive to get the customers to come.

Open days can be an expensive way of getting a new message across, but often the fact you're making contacts and meeting people face-to-face can help build good working relationships.

WAYS TO GIVE AND GET INFORMATION

How to write a business letter
There is an art to writing letters and you should ensure yours are professionally laid out in the company's style. The grammar you use and how you spell words will have an impact on the person who receives the letter. You should be careful not to commit yourself to things you can't deliver. Once it's in writing it is more difficult to change.

There are two types of letter used in business:

- standard
- individual.

Standard letter
Most companies have several letters at the ready on computer. They are made up of the bones of a reply and with a bit of manipulating they give a standard response in an individualised way. There are vacant spaces for addition of name, address and subject as well as any other relevant information. (See Figure 19.)

Individual letter
Often an individual reply is needed if there is a problem, a query or you have to answer questions. See the example in Figure 20.

Tips for writing letters: Look in the files for previously written letters. Look at each paragraph and see how they have phrased it. Borrow their layout. Even borrow their words if they fit the meaning of your own letter.

Layout of a letter
Follow your company layout if they have a set format. An accepted NVQ layout is detailed in Figure 21.

Real Draft Ale = RDA
What has beer got to do with writing letters? Not a lot. But the initials will help you remember how the first part of a letter is laid out:

R Reference
D Date
A Address of person the letter is to.

Salutation
Dear Sir   Dear Madam   Dear Mr Hanson   etc.

The opening paragraph
The first paragraph should be an introduction. Look at the examples you've found in the files. Look at the way the paragraph begins. Does it say:

- 'Thank you for your letter.'

Ferry Electronics

Admiral House, High Street, Fareham PO16 7BB
Tel: 01329 825805

Our ref: VS/SEP/123

Date as postmark

Dear

Thank you for your enquiry.

Enclosed are the information leaflets you requested together with an up-to-date price list.

Please do not hesitate to contact us again should you require any further information.

Yours faithfully

V Shawyer
Sales Co-ordinator

Encs

Fig. 19. Standard reply letter.

Ferry Electrics

Admiral House, High Street, Fareham PO16 7BB
Tel: 01329 825805

Our ref: VS/SEP/123

15 April 199-

Mr G Green
Dice Services
17 Forest Road
Waltham Chase
SOUTHAMPTON   SO32 2NA

Dear Mr Green

Further to our telephone conversation regarding the installation work I am pleased to supply the following information:

EMERGENCY LIGHTING

Emergency lighting to the kitchen area will be provided by maintained luminaires, self-contained type with a 3-hour duration.
One fitting to be located centrally of the kitchen and one fitting to each of the two exit doors.

FIRE ALARM

It is intended to extend the fire alarm system from the surrounding area to incorporate two new call points, one to each of the exit doors, one new rate of rise heat detector, located centrally off the kitchen area and one new sounder - all new accessories to match existing.
Wiring to this work will be in FP200 cable coloured red.

Please do not hesitate to contact me should you require any further information.

Yours sincerely

V Shawyer
Sales Co-ordinator

Fig. 20. Individual reply letter.

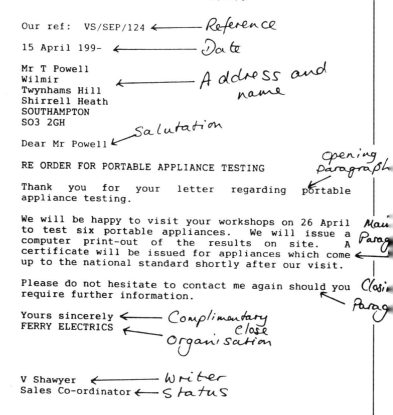

Ferry Electrics

Admiral House, High Street, Fareham PO16 7BB
Tel: 01329 825805

Our ref: VS/SEP/124 ⟵——— *Reference*

15 April 199- ⟵——— *Date*

Mr T Powell
Wilmir
Twynhams Hill ⟵——— *Address and name*
Shirrell Heath
SOUTHAMPTON
SO3 2GH

Salutation

Dear Mr Powell ⟵

RE ORDER FOR PORTABLE APPLIANCE TESTING   *Opening Paragraph*

Thank you for your letter regarding portable
appliance testing.

We will be happy to visit your workshops on 26 April   *Main*
to test six portable appliances.   We will issue a   *Parag*
computer print-out of the results on site.   A
certificate will be issued for appliances which come ⟵
up to the national standard shortly after our visit.

Please do not hesitate to contact me again should you   *Closi*
require further information.   *Parag*

Yours sincerely ⟵——— *Complimentary Close*
FERRY ELECTRICS ⟵——— *Organisation*

V Shawyer ⟵——— *Writer*
Sales Co-ordinator ⟵——— *Status*

Fig. 21. Detailed letter layout.

- 'With reference to your telephone call of...'

- 'Further to your enquiry...'

- 'Many thanks for your order received on...'

- 'Please find enclosed...'

Does it say something else? If it does, would it suit your letter better than any of the above?

The second paragraph
This is the main paragraph (sometimes it's more than one paragraph) which gives details of what the letter is really about:

- 'I am sorry you were disappointed with our product and that you require a refund...'

- 'I am pleased to inform you that we were able to find the book you requested. We will be forwarding it to you shortly.'

- 'The cable you requested is now in stock and we will be despatching it to you within the next few days.'

- 'As you can see from the brochure, we are able to offer very competitive rates on all makes of guitar.'

Closing paragraph
The last paragraph is the finish of the letter and must close it properly:

- 'As a gesture of goodwill I have pleasure in enclosing a refund plus a free sample of one of our other products. Please do not hesitate to contact me should you require further assistance.'

- 'I look forward to receiving your cheque for £9.50 in the near future.'

- 'Please let me know if we can be of further assistance to you in the near future.'

- 'I look forward to receiving your order in the near future.'

Cows
Like real draft ale, cows don't have a lot to do with letter writing, but the initials can help you remember how to finish a letter:

C *Complimentary close*
- 'Yours sincerely' if you know the name of the person you're writing to.
- 'Yours faithfully' if you don't.

O *Organisation name* – in capital letters
e.g. FAREPORT TRAINING ORGANISATION LTD. Leave enough space here to fit in a signature – at least four or five clear lines.

W *Writer* – the name of the person writing the letter.

S *Status of the writer* – who is he/she? Sales, Manager, Customer Service Manager, etc.

Enclosure
If you are enclosing anything with your letter, you should put 'Enc' at the very bottom of your letter (Encs if there is more than one enclosure).

Checking your letter for errors
When you've finished the letter check it through carefully. If you've typed it on a computer, print it out on scrap paper. Manually check it and look for:

1.	Spelling errors	Febuary (February), acomodation (accommodation), etc.
2.	Punctuation errors	Thank-you = thank you, the companys policy = the company's policy.
3.	Grammar errors	'We don't think what you've said is correct.' Should be 'We believe you may have made a mistake.'
4.	Content errors	Is the information you're passing on incorrect – wrong dates, wrong prices, etc?
5.	Missing information	Have you left anything out? Is there supposed to be a price but it's missing?
6.	Unanswered questions	If the letter is a reply, check the original again to see if there are any questions you've failed to answer.
7.	Confidential information	Have you included something you shouldn't have? If you're in any doubt, check with a more senior member of staff.

8. Address   Finally, recheck the name and address to
                          make sure it's correct.

Hints and tips on using the telephone

When someone calls you:

• It's the fashion to use a person's name during the conversation as it makes them feel important. It also helps you remember who you're speaking to.

• Avoid using slang including the word 'OK'.

• Say figures in pairs as they're easier to understand, e.g. 'fifty-three' rather than 'five three'.

• Ask the caller to repeat anything you didn't quite catch. Ask them to spell difficult names.

• Check all the main points you've discussed before ringing off, including names, dates, figures, etc.

• If you end the call finish by saying 'thank you for calling'.

When you make the call:

• Before you dial write down all the things you want to know. Give yourself enough room to write the answers beside.

• Check the number you're going to dial.

• As soon as you get through check you have the right place. Ask for the person you want to contact.

• When you're asked 'who's calling?' speak clearly and precisely.

• When your contact comes on the line greet them properly. Make it clear if you're phoning on behalf of someone else.

• Speak clearly when you state the facts you have previously made a note of.

• Make notes as the person responds. Don't scrawl but write legibly so you can read your own notes.

• Summarise the main points at the end of the conversation so that it's clear you haven't misunderstood or missed out any details.

• As you made the call, conclude the conversation at your end.

- If you made the call on behalf of someone else, write a memo or report to summarise the information and pass it to them immediately.

Confidentiality
Don't talk about something private in front of other people. One-way conversations are quite easy to misinterpret or to get the gist of what is being said.

Two-way communication
Sharing information with your customer should always be a two-way thing. Don't waste their time and always consider the quickest way to deal with any problem. Use whichever method of communication is most suited to the particular occasion.

Problems in information flow
If you have a problem when communicating with a customer, get help. Talk about it to your colleagues. Together you may be able to sort it out, especially if you aren't in the position to be able to make decisions at a higher level.

What other ways do we give and get information?
As well as the three traditional methods of communicating, i.e. face-to-face, telephone and in writing, there is another way: body language. Check out Chapter 3 to remind yourself how important this is.

Don't keep customers in the dark
Customers should always be kept informed about what you intend to do to help them. If you say you're going to write to them with more details you should keep your promise. If you say you'll ring them tomorrow, do it. If you ask them to come back next week, make sure you're in the office or shop.

Don't treat customers like idiots
When you speak to a customer don't talk down to them, act in an over-familiar manner or try to impress them by using language they don't understand. Similarly, don't send out a badly written letter or one that will confuse or annoy them. Always think carefully about what you want to get across and how best to do this with the particular customer you're dealing with.

Remember – all customers are individuals. The methods you used last week for a bank manager might not be appropriate for a small child.

Similarly, if you are dealing with someone with a learning or physical disability or perhaps they come from another country or a different area, you may need to write things down, draw diagrams, speak more clearly. Watch their body language to see if you're getting through.

Regularly check with your customer to make sure they understand what you're telling them. Watch their facial expression:

- Are their eyes showing signs of boredom?

- Do they look confused?

Ask them questions, give them time to ask you questions, ask if they need more information. Don't assume they have understood you the first time.

If you are still having problems, remember the other members of your team are there to back you up. Watch how they deal with problems and pick up tips on how they managed to get the message across when you didn't.

COLLECTING EVIDENCE FOR YOUR NVQ

Listed below are a few examples of evidence you can collect for the following NVQ Elements:

Customer Service Level 3
Element: 2.1   2.2   2.3

- Examples of brochures, magazines and information leaflets on your product/service.

- Circulation slips.

- Memos or notes from other staff informing them of a new product, service or information on a customer.

- Customer feedback log.

- Report on a new innovation.

- Company procedures on selecting information for communication to customers.

- A flow chart to show flow of information to customers and from customers.

- Minutes of meetings which pass on information about new

products and/or services as well as changes to systems of delivering customer service.

- Copies of advertisements in local papers or *Yellow Pages.*

- Invitations to customers to visit showroom, warehouse or office.

- A case study (see Chapter 9).

- Witness statements from colleagues/customers.

CHECKLIST

Level 3 Element 2.1   **Select information for communication to customer**

Performance criteria	Can do	Need more experience	Need training
(a) Do you regularly examine information leaflets and documents which are relevant to your customers?			
(b) Can you identify how your customers feel about a problem? Do you check with them and acknowledge you understand their view in all communications?			
(c) Do you consider your customers' needs when you give information, ensuring it is accurate, relevant, complete and promptly given?			
(d) Do you tell your customers about products or services which you know will meet their needs?			
(e) Do you give information to your customers in such a way that it causes them as little worry as possible?			
(f) Do you file information which may be of future interest to your customers in an appropriate place where it can be found easily?			

Level 3 Element 2.2   **Improve the flow of information between organisation and customer**

Performance criteria	Can do	Need more experience	Need training
(a) Does the information you both give and draw from your customers help you progress towards meeting their needs? Is this done within an acceptable timescale from the customers' point of view?			
(b) Does the way you communicate with your customers make best use of their time?			
(c) Do you promptly communicate with your customers face-to-face, in writing or by telephone, using methods you are used to?			
(d) Do you try to develop new opportunities to communicate with your customers and use them when the occasion arises?			
(e) Do you discuss the customers' problems you've identified with colleagues, especially those in a position to help solve them?			

Level 3 Element 2.3 **Adapt methods of communication to customers**

Performance criteria	Can do	Need more experience	Need training
(a) Do you adapt and use different types of communication to keep customers informed about what you are currently doing, or hope to do, to help solve their problems?			
(b) Do you adapt your language, written or spoken, to suit the individual customer?			
(c) Do you adapt the way you communicate with customers with individual needs, e.g. physical/learning disabilities and language differences?			
(d) Do you regularly check your customer understands what you are trying to communicate to them?			
(e) Do you openly acknowledge when you are out of your depth and seek help from others to help solve the problem?			

CASE STUDIES

Bryan hogs the magazines

A quarterly canoeing magazine arrives at the Centre for the attention of Bryan. It is paid for by the Centre but Bryan looks on it as his own. He doesn't pass it around as he is worried the activity staff will ruin the cover.

It's a busy month and he fails to read the magazine in which there is an article about the River Authority and new rules concerning controls for canoeists. If he had circulated it someone else may have spotted it.

Only when he plans an expedition for a group of managers does Bryan come across a problem with the particular stretch of water he plans to use.

Virginia helps with the open day

Virginia is helping the Director to plan an Open Day. He intends to advertise on Radio Solent as well as Meridian Television.

Invitations will be extended to anyone in the south of England who would like to sample an activity at a reduced cost. He is hoping the day will help pay for the new climbing tower as well as bring in new business.

Kelly adapts her language

Kelly is dealing with a school group from France. They are all quite fluent in English. She speaks slowly and clearly and finds they can understand everything she says.

When a youth group from Scotland arrives she assumes she won't have to make a special effort. However, after a while she realises she's speaking too quickly for them to pick up what she's saying.

DISCUSSION POINTS

1. Have you dealt with a customer with individual needs (physical/ learning disability or language difference)? Do you think you dealt with them in a way you yourself would like to be treated if the roles were reversed?

2. Think about what it is that you do and don't like about certain people. Do you think they know how you feel? If so, what can you do to avoid bad feeling in the future?

3. Does your company buy magazines or newspapers relating to your particular business? If so, which have you seen this month and did you read them?

7
Solving Problems for Customers

FINDING OUT WHAT'S GONE WRONG

Why?

Before you can solve a problem on behalf of a customer you have to find out what's gone wrong. If there's a problem – what is it? If the customer's unhappy – why?

- Are they being unreasonable?

- Do they have a genuine gripe?

- Is the problem one that's occurred before?

- Is this something completely new to you?

What if the feedback's personal?

If you get feedback from a customer and it relates to something you can deal with yourself – the way you handle an item, the way you answer the telephone, etc. – do something to improve things straightaway. Don't ignore their comments even if you're not happy with them.

Example

Jane is working in her friend's shop as a favour. She has just served a customer. The customer holds out his hand for his change and Jane places it directly into his palm without counting it out.

' 'Scuse me, love,' he says, 'I think you're new to this. Mind if I show you how to count out change before someone makes a complaint.' He tries to be light-hearted but Jane is annoyed that he should even mention the matter to her. She's doing her mate a favour, for God's sake. She bites her tongue and allows him to show her.

When he leaves the shop she curses him and calls him a few choice names. However, when the next customer comes in she finds herself counting out the change!

116

Listening to an angry customer

If a customer is really angry or upset, your first task is to let them have their say. If you gaze impatiently around the shop or office and they think you're not interested they will continue to be angry.

Next, try to calm them down. If they are emotionally charged they won't hear what you're saying anyway.

Sounds easy. But we all know when human feelings and emotions are involved it might be a lot more complicated.

DANGER: what you *shouldn't* do

- Make a decision there and then without thinking about the problem carefully.

- Assume you know the answer because it's happened before.

- Assume you need to know everything before you can begin to help. If you wait to find out all the facts it may be too late to do anything anyway.

- Think you can handle it on your own without anyone else's help. It's always better to talk it through with your colleagues.

- Try to solve every problem customers throw at you. Some problems sort themselves out. Some problems need to be directed to other people immediately. Your job is to know the difference.

Questioning

You may have to question the customer but be sensitive and once you understand what the problem is, acknowledge it:

- Is it that the product or service isn't obviously available?

- Is it the quality of the product or the service they've received?

- Is it how to use the product or service they've bought or are interested in buying?

- Is it about the company – about their systems or the way they do things?

- Is it a complaint about a member of staff?

Gathering information

Make enquiries and gather as much information as you can. Talk to your colleagues to see if they have any information about the problem. Get more information from the customer or from other sources if necessary.

- Do you need information from inside or outside the organisation?

- Is it easy to collect through the normal channels?

- Does the matter need further investigation?

See Figure 22 for examples of sources of information.

1.   Your own memory or written notes.
2.   Other people in your line of business – inside or outside of your organisation.
3.   Leaflets and brochures.
4.   Information held on computer, including the World Wide Web, New Prestel, Electronic Yellow Pages, etc.
5.   Information held in the filing system.
6.   Newspapers.
7.   Magazines and journals.
8.   Reference books.
9.   Local organisations, e.g. Chamber of Commerce, Post Office, Citizens Advice Bureau, etc.
10.   National organisations, e.g. trade association, Tourist Information Offices, etc.

Fig. 22. Where to get information.

Summarising your information
Once you've found out as much as you can, summarise the problem. Write it down if it helps to clarify it in your own head.

Work out what your priorities are – what action should you take first?

Think about your customer. Are they worried? Are they unhappy? Think carefully how you respond to protect them from further worry.

If the problem or complaint is something that's happened before, pass the information on to your supervisor or someone in authority who can do something about it.

Problem-solving grid

The grid below is one way to help you think about a problem. On the
left are prompts, on the right a fictitious problem. You could try the
same method if you come across a real problem of your own.

Setting the scene	**Write down *all* the facts**
Who's involved?	Me, Bill, Miriam, Barbara, Rosemary, my director, Mick. Two customer who made a complaint.
What happened?	Barbara is my trainee. I've put her on Reception because Rosemary's off this week. Barbara usually does jobs for other people. Now she's on Reception Bill and Miriam think they can still ask her to do tasks for them. The problem started when Miriam asked Barbara to go to the shop for her. Because she usually does this, Barbara went up the road, leaving Reception unattended. Two customers arrived and had to wait ten minutes before anyone knew they were there. They made a complaint to the Director.
Who is it affecting?	My Director is really annoyed because the two customers were important. Even though they're senior to me I was so angry at being blamed for the customers' complaint I had a go at Miriam and Bill. Now they're not speaking to me.
Has it happened before?	No. I've never put a trainee on the Reception desk before?
Any other facts?	Barbara's confused and now hates it on Reception. It's affecting our customers. They've not only complained to my boss that it took so long to be seen, but others have complained about the way Barbara answers the telephone now.

What happened?	Write down *all* the facts
Why did it happen?	I had some urgent letters I wanted Barbara to post and I couldn't find her. When I heard she was up the road buying some milk for Miriam I wasn't too pleased. When I tried to find Barbara later she was photocopying for Bill. When my boss phoned to complain that visitors have been left waiting in Reception, I was livid.
Why do I feel angry/annoyed?	Because no one asked if they could get Barbara to do tasks for them. I'm also annoyed because she's my trainee and I need to know where she is because she's my responsibility. They don't seem to realise her job role has changed this week.
Why do Bill and Miriam feel angry?	I expect it was the way I spoke to them. I was a bit hot under the collar and was quite sharp and rude.
Why is Barbara not answering the phone properly?	She's worried she's upset Bill and Miriam. She usually gets on well with everyone in the office. I know she's worried about the complaints we've received from our customers.
Analyse the situation	**Write down *all* the facts**
Were you to blame?	Partly. I lost my temper. I should have thought about the situation before confronting Bill and Miriam. I should have also told them about Barbara's new responsibilities. They didn't know she was on her own in Reception because it's on a different floor from them.
Were others to blame?	Bill and Miriam knew Barbara was under my supervision. They shouldn't have given her jobs without talking to me about it first. Normally they do as she's usually located in my office. Barbara shouldn't have left Reception unattended.

Were innocent parties involved?	The customers couldn't understand why there was no one to greet them in Reception. The Director got involved because the customers complained to him.
What should you do?	I should talk to my manager, Ann, and tell her what happened. I know I have to sort it out myself, but it's affecting our customers and the Director is angry.

What will you do?   **Write down *all* the facts**

First action	Talk to Barbara. She's still on Reception as we are short of staff and there's no one to take over. Apologise for putting her in the position I did and for not telling the staff about the change in her role. Explain why it's necessary to always cover Reception. Tell her the complaint wasn't her problem and that she's doing really well. Encourage her and build up her confidence again by sitting with her for a while until she's answered a few phone calls. Praise her again. Finally, offer to cover Reception if she needs to take a break.
Second action	Talk to Bill and Miriam. Apologise for my outburst. Explain why it happened. Explain about Barbara's new role and apologise for not letting them know. Hopefully, they will accept my apology.
Third action	Write a report on what happened and what I've done about it. Give a copy each to my manager and the Director and keep a copy in my file. Offer to apologise to the customers.

DECIDING WHAT TO DO

Sometimes it's better to do nothing if the problem doesn't need immediate attention. Some problems cure themselves – others are made worse if we interfere. However, if the problem is more complex you will need to act. Experience will help you recognise which category your problem falls into.

We have ways of dealing with complaints

Your company will have procedures for dealing with a complaint if it is genuine:

- chasing up a supplier
- suggesting a different product or service
- exchanging faulty goods
- offering a refund
- issuing a credit
- carrying out a repair job free of charge
- offering an apology
- giving a free item as a gesture of goodwill
- changing systems so it doesn't happen again.

Don't wait until there's a problem to find out what your company's procedures are.

Making changes

Making small changes won't affect other people. But if you change something based on feedback from customers, whether it's a new form you've designed or a different way of doing things, if it's been passed by your supervisor you need to let other people know about it. Don't assume that your supervisor will do this. They may have OK'd its introduction but they may also assume that you will inform other people about it.

Formal? Informal? Which system do you use?

Whatever systems your company operates you must think about them all. If the problem is with a product that's come from an outside supplier, you may need to contact them.

Don't attempt to go to outside regulatory bodies, Trading Standards, Customs and Excise, LAUTRO (Life Assurance and Unit Trust Regulatory Organisation), Health and Safety Executive, etc., without first discussing it with management. It's OK using your initiative but you must also keep others informed. They may know something you don't.

Informal example
Someone complains about a packet of sweets they've bought pointing out they're out-of-date. You're the only one in the shop and have to make a decision. You offer to exchange the packet immediately and apologise for the inconvenience.

You tell your supervisor about it later and explain you've also removed the remainder of the out-of-date packets.

Formal example
You get a phone call from a customer complaining about the work one of your fitters has done. You take all the details and explain you will get your manager to call them as soon as he comes in. You know you can't deal with this on your own and you must go through more formal channels.

Being flexible
We've all heard of the 'It's-more-than-my-job's-worth' syndrome when someone is so stubborn and inflexible they would rather do nothing than try to help if it is slightly outside their understanding of the rules and regulations.

Be flexible and do everything you can to benefit the customer rather than get in his/her way. It may be that the way you've handled something before is no longer appropriate. Maybe you need to consider a different way to help solve the current or future problems.

ACTING ON YOUR DECISION

Don't try offloading the responsibility to act on your decision. If it's your problem you should deliver the solution yourself.

- Whether the procedures you use to do this are standard or not, you should act promptly.

- No matter where you got your information from, if you discover the problem is something which has happened before – and is likely to happen again – pass it on to the correct person so that something can be done to stop it happening again. Write a report if necessary or a memo to the appropriate person.

- Pass on details of how you sorted out the problem. It may be of help to someone in the future if the situation arises again. It should also be recorded in the customer's file for future reference.

- Don't just leave it and think you have solved everything. Check the situation again to make sure the problem doesn't recur. If you can see there is still a problem, whether it's going to affect you or your colleagues, whether it's a problem with a product or with a staff member, don't keep it to yourself.

- When you take actions think carefully about how to communicate them:
  - Is it better to talk to the customer face-to-face?
  - Should you write them a letter?
  - Would it be better to telephone them straightaway and then follow up the conversation with a letter?

- If you haven't been able to solve the problem in the way the customer expected you to, make sure you present an alternative method in as positive a way as possible.

- The customer may ask for your advice but if you don't know the answer don't fob them off with something you're unsure of. Tell them where they can get the information or advice and give them a phone number or address of the outside organisation if you have it.

COLLECTING EVIDENCE FOR YOUR NVQ

Listed below are a few examples of evidence you can collect for the following NVQ Elements:

Customer Service Level 2   **Level 3**
Element: 4.1 4.2 4.3   **4.1 4.2 4.3**

- Brochures and information leaflets on your product/service.

- Letters from customers thanking you for your help.

- Job allocation chart, work schedule, bookings diary, etc.

- Memos or notes from other staff asking you to deal with a customer.

- A flow chart to show the channels you need to go through to resolve a problem when things go wrong.

- An organisation chart.

- Minutes of meetings where your name is mentioned as delivering good customer service.

- Your job description.

- A case study (see Chapter 9).

- Witness statements from colleagues/customers.

CHECKLIST

Level 2 Element 4.1   **Gather information on customer problems**

Performance criteria	Can do	Need more experience	Need training
(a) Do you find out exactly what the customer thinks the problem is? Are you sensitive when you acknowledge what this is?			
(b) Do you use the information gained from customers to help you clarify and summarise their problems?			
(c) Do you consult colleagues for information relating to the problems which are affecting your customers?			
(d) Do you make note of information about recurring problems or complaints? Do you pass the details to the people who can help solve them?			

Level 2 Element 4.2   **Propose solutions for customers**

Performance criteria	Can do	Need more experience	Need training
(a) Do you ask your colleagues for help to solve customer problems?			
(b) Do you look for current formal and informal ways to help solve a customer problem?			
(c) Do you suggest other products or services which may help to solve a customer problem?			
(d) Do you make sure the customer understands what you are proposing and why?			

Level 2 Element 4.3   **Take action to deliver solutions**

Performance criteria	Can do	Need more experience	Need training
(a) Do you promptly begin procedures to find the answers to customers' problems?			
(b) Do you check the way you deliver your service and pass on to the appropriate person details of any problems arising?			
(c) Do you carry out solutions to customer problems with the help and co-operation of others?			
(d) Do you take action within your own area of authority to prevent shortfalls in the delivery of products or services, whether they are to do with you or from somewhere else?			
(e) Do you take action to alert colleagues about potential shortfalls in delivery of products or services?			

Level 3 Element 4.1   **Identify and interpret problems affecting customers**

Performance criteria	Can do	Need more experience	Need training
(a) Do you understand how a customer sees the problem? Do you question them and sensitively acknowledge their feelings?			
(b) Do you gather and systematically analyse and prioritise information gathered about the customer's problem?			
(c) Can you clearly summarise customers' problems using the information you've gained from them as well as your perceptions or gut reactions?			
(d) Is the way you react to the problem designed to protect customers from unnecessary worry?			

Level 3 Element 4.2   **Generate solutions on behalf of customers**

Performance criteria	Can do	Need more experience	Need training
(a) Do you examine all the different ways you can to try to find an answer to customer problems?			
(b) Do you seek advice from people inside your organisation, outside suppliers and regulatory bodies to find answers to customer problems?			
(c) Do you look at formal and informal ways to find answers to customer problems? Are you flexible when you look at these ways?			
(d) Do you look for alternative ways to find answers which will benefit the customer the most?			
(e) Do you look for new ways to solve problems including changing/modifying current ways or adding new ones? Do you agree these with the appropriate people in your company?			

Performance criteria	Can do	Need more experience	Need training
(a) Do you promptly begin procedures to find the answers to customers' problems?			
(b) Do you immediately pass on clear information about recurring problems and complaints to the right person in your company?			
(c) Do you immediately pass clear information about how you're going to solve the problem to the right person in your company?			
(d) Do you keep an eye on how you deliver solutions? Do you modify them if you see a problem arising?			
(e) Do you think about how you're going to communicate with your customers, e.g. face-to-face, in writing or by telephone?			
(f) If you know there is a problem with your solution, do you positively offer an alternative way of dealing with the situation to the customer?			
(g) Do you give customers accurate advice about alternative ways to solve their problems if these are outside your own organisation?			

CASE STUDIES

Virginia receives a request

An inner city group from Paddington have asked Virginia if she can organise a canoeing expedition with overnight bivouac as an addition to their programme. Several of their group have developed a great love for the water and their leader hopes to give them something they will always remember.

Bryan rearranges the programme

Virginia discusses the group's request with Bryan and explains how important she thinks the change will be for the group. He can see her point of view and checks the staffing rota.

There are few staff available so he decides to lead the expedition himself. He programmes Lee and Carina as his assistants.

As the predominantly Afro-Caribbean group prepare to depart there is an air of excitement amongst them which is more than contagious.

Lee and Carina work together

It isn't often Lee and Carina get the chance to work together. It is also the first time they've worked with Bryan. As the expedition progresses they see a totally different side to him. They realise he isn't all bad and the overnight sleep-out helps to unite them as a staff team.

DISCUSSION POINTS

1. Does your company have guidelines on how to solve problems on behalf of the customer? If they do, have you read them? If they don't, who would you approach to suggest the procedures were written up?

2. Does your company have special forms for crediting goods or services? Where are these kept, do you know how to complete them and what do you do with them after completion?

3. How flexible are you? If you know your company's systems do you know exactly how far you can go outside these to solve a problem before seeking help from a supervisor or manager?

8
Making Changes to
Improve Service

LISTENING CAREFULLY TO COMPLAINTS

Improving your service

Wise companies take note of their customers' comments and act on them – by improving a poor service, changing an unpopular line, expanding on something that's popular or praising a staff member who's done a particularly good job.

There are many companies who operate an incentive scheme and big prizes can be won by staff who excel in their job. If they don't listen to their customers, however, there's little chance of knowing what they're doing right – or wrong.

Methods of collecting information

Not many people write letters of thanks these days. If they do they should be circulated to the people concerned and stored in a special file. The information should be used together with other feedback information.

Feedback is much more likely to come from a comment from a customer in person or when they are talking to you on the telephone. Once the comment has been made it is often lost in infinity.

Having a feedback log – placed in a central, easy-to-locate place – which is used by all staff will give a fuller picture of how your organisation is seen through the eyes of the customer. The importance of such a log should be stressed to the staff and they should get into the habit of filling it in. (See Figure 23.)

Formal method of collecting information

Another way to collect feedback information from customers is to display feedback forms in the reception area, on wall displays, etc. and invite people to complete and return them to you as soon as possible. You could also send survey forms to customers after specific events or special offers.

CUSTOMER FEEDBACK

Please give details of any customer feedback. If further action was taken or a report written please acknowledge this on the form:

Date	Customer name, address, tele no.	Details of feedback	Dealt with by	Info passed to	See Report	(a)	(b)
25.7.9-	Peter Dimmock Gosport 381521	Not happy with light fitting (fitter-John)	Shaun P	Gordon G	REP. 0163		✓
2.8.9-	Mr Cann Locks Head 748610	Cables not finished properly (fitter-John)	Shaun P	" — "	REP. 0164		✓
5.8.9-	Supersave Fareham 281762	Left place clean & tidy (fitter-Ray)	Shaun P	" — "	REP. 0165	✓	
10.8.9-	Four Posts Eng. Fareham 814672	Shoddy job (fitter-John)	Shaun P	" — "	REP. 0165		✓

(a) - Commendation
(b) - Complaint

Fig. 23. Customer feedback log.

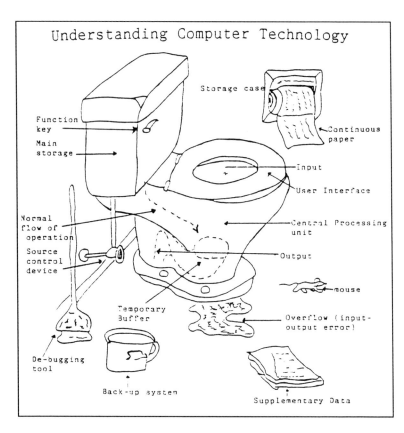

Fig. 24. Pictorial information.

SALES: JANUARY – APRIL 199X

Month	Sales: Hardware £	Sales: Electrical £	Sales: Furnish £	Total
January	1,345	4,341	5,431	11,117
February	1,467	2,226	3,545	7,238
March	1,632	2,464	3,212	7,308
April	1,378	3,211	4,321	8,910
TOTAL	5,822	12,242	16,509	34,573

Fig. 25. Table.

These more formal methods of collecting information give you the opportunity to gather details you're particularly interested in. However, if the form is too long or too complicated you may not encourage your customer to return it.

Putting it together
Once you've collected the information you should put it together and somehow display it. The method used should be the easiest to understand for the particular type of information.

Ways to display information

Textual
This could be typed or written and can be a summary of facts or a more in-depth report. It must be accurate and neatly displayed, easy to read and clear.

Graphical
There are several different types of graphical display:

- diagrams
- flow charts
- pie charts
- line graphs
- bar charts.

All are quick and easy to interpret – as long as there is a 'key' to tell you what the sections represent.

Graphs can tell you at a glance what is popular, what is unpopular, what months are the busiest, when the slack periods are. They can also highlight weaknesses in staff support or if someone is under-performing.

Pictorial
Newspapers often use pictures to illustrate a particular point. Cartoons make us make us laugh but also send us messages (see Figure 24).

Tabular
A table or tab is an easy-to-understand method of giving information. It can clearly highlight differences while giving precise figures as well (see Figure 25).

Obtaining and analysing feedback

Finally, bear these points in mind when you are obtaining and analysing feedback from your customers:

- Find out how your customers feel about the service or goods you offer them. Ignorance isn't bliss in business.

- Use the formal and informal complaints or praise you receive to judge whether or not you are giving your customers what they want.

- Think of new ways to obtain customer feedback. Don't sit and wait for it to come – it might not happen.

- More formally, work with other staff to produce a customer survey form and make sure it gets to the people it's aimed at.

- Analyse the information you get whether it's gathered by your own efforts or through an organised survey. Look for patterns and trends. See where the high and low points are. Put the information together in a form that others will find easy to understand.

- Present your findings to your supervisor or manager. Give copies to staff who will benefit from the information. If it's to go into a report, file it where you know you can lay your hands on it quickly.

DECIDING IF IMPROVEMENTS ARE NEEDED

Proposals

Once all the information has been gathered, analysed and presented, you then have to decide whether any improvements to your customer service delivery are needed. If you decide they are, you then have to put your proposals to your manager and/or others in your company who are in a position to authorise the changes.

- If the changes have been initiated by yourself or someone else they must be presented professionally.

- Proposed changes must be based on accurate information and contain all the facts as clearly set out as possible.

- Predict your customers' requirements based on the facts and figures you've collected from their feedback. Accurately interpret the information to help you look into the future. The forecasts you make should take into account both the quality and quantity of service and goods.

- The information gathered from inside and outside the company, whether routinely or non-routinely sought, must be summarised accurately. The way you present the information should show why you have made certain proposals to improve customer service.

- It must be passed to the right person, whether it's your manager or someone else in authority in your company, who can make the decision to go ahead with the changes.

Note: You don't always need to carry out surveys or ask customers' opinions to see there's a problem, but you do still need to feedback your observations to your supervisor.

Quantitative and qualitative
There seem to be certain words which are fashionable in NVQ circles. The above are two of them.

Qualitative = quality
When predicting how to improve your services and what the customers' future requirements are you could use qualitative methods. To do this you have to find out exactly what customers think about the overall good or bad qualities of service or goods offered by your company.

- It could be the quality of the workmanship over a period of time. Did a fitter do a good job on one occasion even though his work is generally poor? The lucky customer he pleased might think he's brilliant but would the other customers he's worked for?

- It could be the quality of the service a customer receives from counter staff. Are they always polite, sometimes polite, never polite? Do they immediately serve you, still gas to their friends when you arrive, ignore you until they're ready?

- It could be the quality of sand you've bought from a builders' merchant. Is the quality usually good, have you occasionally had a poor batch, is it generally of low quality?

To produce a qualitative graph
The figures you collect from feedback must be taken over a period of time. It would be unfair to use a short period – we all have bad days, farmers have dry weather and sometimes crops are poor, factories have supply problems which cause a blip in production. (See Figure 26.).

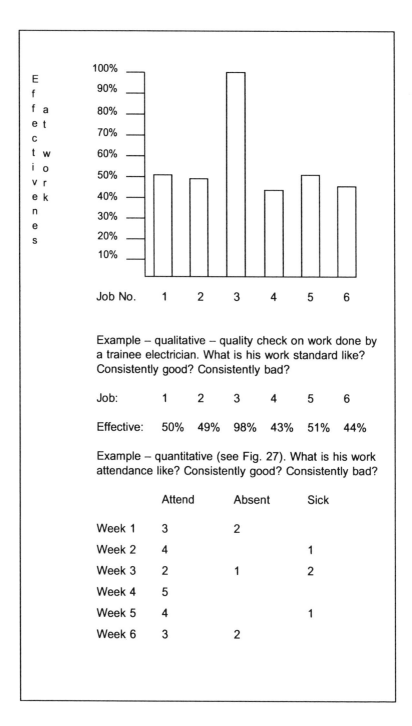

Example – qualitative – quality check on work done by a trainee electrician. What is his work standard like? Consistently good? Consistently bad?

Job:	1	2	3	4	5	6
Effective:	50%	49%	98%	43%	51%	44%

Example – quantitative (see Fig. 27). What is his work attendance like? Consistently good? Consistently bad?

	Attend	Absent	Sick
Week 1	3	2	
Week 2	4		1
Week 3	2	1	2
Week 4	5		
Week 5	4		1
Week 6	3	2	

Fig. 26. Qualitative graph.

Quantitative = quantity
When predicting using quantitative methods you are not only finding
out about the quality but how many times it has been good or bad.
You could also be seeking feedback to find out how many products of
a certain line have been sold.

- How many tins of baked beans have you sold this month? Which
  are selling better? The cheaper brands or the more expensive?

- How many customers have asked for a certain hairdresser to cut
  their hair? Do people prefer to use another hairdresser when they
  have a perm? Why?

- Will a new yoghurt sell? You set up a table and give free samples to
  your customers as they come in. You ask them what they think of
  it. Fifty say they'd buy it. Ten say they wouldn't. The quantity of
  interested shoppers warrants the product being stocked.

To produce a quantitative graph
Again, the figures you collect from feedback *must* be taken over a
period of time. There are always fluctuations in how often a service is
used or goods bought – in hot weather salads are more popular than
in the winter, bank holidays bring out hoards of DIY fans whereas
sales of solid fuel go up in autumn.

MAKING NECESSARY CHANGES

Who takes the action?
Assuming you've collected accurate feedback from your customers,
found out what they like and don't like, taken the details to someone
who can authorise doing something about it, it's time to make any
necessary changes.

Some actions can be taken by you or you may be asked to carry
them out. Some can be dealt with without making any difference to
anyone else in the organisation – perhaps moving a display which
customers keep walking into. Others may be from a department head
– buying a new line of goods, buying more of another, dropping
something else. Others could include changing a form or producing a
new one, starting a complaints book or a Reception register.

Staffing problems
The change may relate to a staff member's personal performance.
They may be giving the company a bad name.

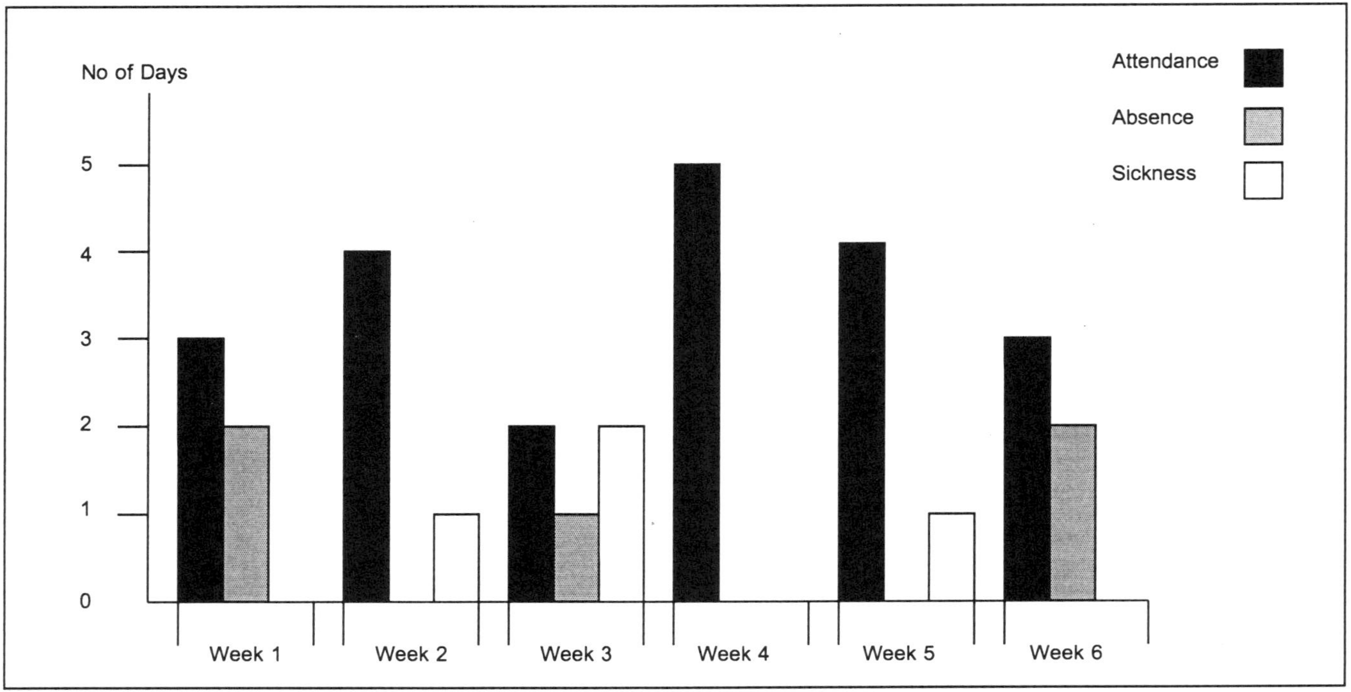

Fig. 27. Quantitative graph.

138

- They could be offered another chance if they've had a personal problem.

- Perhaps they need training if their skills are rusty/non-existent (people do lie about their experience/qualifications).

- They may be given an official warning and ultimately sacked.

Changes in procedures

Some actions are taken to the Board, discussed at a meeting or added to the official company procedures.

If you've been asked to make changes or you've taken the initiative yourself, and if the changes affect other members of staff, they must be informed by word-of-mouth or in writing (both if possible as people sometimes forget what they've been told if they're distracted or busy with something else).

The changes should be a response to the customers' requirements and not your own personal requirements. Don't overstep your authority. Change only the things you've been authorised to do, whether they are:

- regarding the things you sell or the services you offer

- changes to the rules and regulations about how you or other staff are expected to work and the targets you should come up to

- about training yourself or the staff to provide a better customer service

- of concern to other departments because they affect them as well

- related to the suppliers you use.

Changes introduced by others

If the changes have been introduced by someone else you should support and help them by using your own experience and ideas to make the changes successful. For instance, if you are particularly good at using the graphics programme on the computer perhaps you could volunteer to produce a poster to advertise a new line of products. If it's a new company procedure, e.g. keeping a mileage log, you should try to make the system work by completing yours.

IS IT REALLY AN IMPROVEMENT?

Admitting when things don't work

Not all changes are improvements. It is only when you try something out that you know whether or not it's going to work. Never be afraid to admit your idea isn't working. You can always go back to the old way or think of something different.

Cost-effective?

Think of the cost. Is the change costing the company money? Will the benefits outweigh any initial expenses?

Whether the changes are to do with the way you work, the systems you use, or the products or services your company supply, remember to work as a team. Let your manager or others in your organisation know if the changes are working or not. Your feedback may involve comments on new company procedures, a new product or service you're offering, or policy change.

Be constructive and positive. Tell them what you feel is right about the change, or what is wrong. Remember – the idea of making changes is to improve your customer service, not necessarily to benefit you and your job, so don't use the 'feedback' as a bitching session.

COLLECTING EVIDENCE FOR YOUR NVQ

Listed below are a few examples of evidence you can collect for the following NVQ Elements:

Customer Service Level 3
Element: 5.1   5.2   5.3   5.4

- Letters from customers thanking you for your help.

- Letters of complaint – together with details of how you dealt with it.

- Letters of commendation to praise a product or service.

- Feedback journal giving details of complaints and praise over a period of time.

- BS5750 or ISO9002 certificate.

- Company procedures for obtaining feedback.

- Memos or notes from other staff asking you to deal with a customer.

- A flow chart to show the channels you need to go through to resolve a problem when things go wrong.

- Graphs to show quantitative and qualitative predictions.

- Reports on the outcome of the changes.

- New policies written.

- A case study (see Chapter 9).

- Witness statements from colleagues/customers.

CHECKLIST

Level 3 Element 5.1   **Obtain and analyse feedback from customer**

Performance criteria	Can do	Need more experience	Need training
(a) Do you continually seek comments from your customers about your organisation's services?			
(b) Do you use both complaints and commendations from your customers to work out which products and services are successful or otherwise?			
(c) Do you think of new opportunities to gain feedback from customers?			
(d) Do you analyse customer feedback and lay it out in such a way that others can see patterns and trends in the results?			
(e) Do you store customer feedback in the most appropriate place?			

Level 3 Element 5.2 **Propose improvements in service delivery based on customer feedback**

Performance criteria	Can do	Need more experience	Need training
(a) Do you present accurate information on proposed customer service improvements clearly and in the most appropriate form?			
(b) Are your predictions on customer requirements based on an accurate interpretation of customer feedback?			
(c) Do you pass concise information on proposed improvements to the right people inside your organisation?			

Level 3 Element 5.3 **Initiative changes in response to customer requirements**

Performance criteria	Can do	Need more experience	Need training
(a) Do you take action within your own area of authority to remedy shortfalls in customer service?			
(b) Do you take action to alert others to the changes needed to improve customer service?			
(c) Do you introduce your own ideas to respond to customer requirements within your own area of authority?			
(d) Are your actions and ideas based on a thorough analysis of the data you collect? Do you take into account any predicted customer needs?			
(e) Do you use your own ideas and experience to implement changes introduced by others?			

Level 3 Element 5.4   **Evaluate changes designed to improve service to customers**

Performance criteria	Can do	Need more experience	Need training
(a) Do you monitor the outcomes of changes to improve customer service using all the available feedback?			
(b) Do you inform appropriate colleagues of the implications of changes to products and services?			
(c) Do you communicate recommendations on the effectiveness of changes to the appropriate colleagues?			

CASE STUDIES

Next year's brochure

Virginia is interested to know which activities the school groups particularly enjoy. She is trying to put together an advertising brochure for next year and wants to give prominence to the activities which most attract them to the Centre.

She produces a feedback form and with the Director's permission, circulates it to all the groups on the morning of their departure.

Bryan cashes in on the Lottery

From the information Virginia has gathered, Bryan discovers how popular archery has become. The Centre has been given funding from the Lottery and it's his responsibility to make proposals of where part of the money could be put to best use.

As the archery range is becoming fairly dilapidated and the equipment is rather old, he proposes some of the money could be used for that.

Kelly introduces a comments book

Kelly has asked if she can introduce a visitors' comment book. She is given permission to start one and keeps it on the Reception desk.

Visitors are encouraged to make comments when they come to pay their bill. The book soon makes interesting reading and gives the management some idea of what the visitors find good or bad about the Centre.

DISCUSSION POINTS

1. Have you heard comments from customers and not passed them on? Can you see the importance of listening to what people say and not dismissing their comments as just another moaning customer?

2. What systems does your company use to collect customer feedback?

3. Have you had an idea at work which has been buzzing around your head for ages? Talk to one of your colleagues and find out what they think. If they agree it's a good idea, pass it on to your supervisor or manager.

9
Putting Your Customer Service NVQ Together

UNDERSTANDING THE JARGON

Each National Vocational Qualification (NVQ) is made up of two parts:

- the standards
- the competence records (see below, Ways to record evidence).

The standards
These give details of what you have to do to pass the Award. Each standard covers the following:

- *Performance criteria* – how you should perform.
- *Range statements* – the variety of experiences you should have covered.
- *Knowledge* – things you should know about the job.
- *Understanding* – how to do things.
- *Evidence requirements* – what the examiner expects to find in your file.

Each section goes into detail and you will be expected to cover it all. But it's not as bad as it seems as one piece of evidence may cover quite a lot of ground if you think carefully before choosing what you're going to use.

Performance criteria
Each chapter in this book refers to particular elements in the Levels 2 and 3 Customer Service (details under the Checklist sections). The checklists themselves refer directly to the performance criteria. To help you understand the jargon they have been turned into questions.

APL
You can use any previous experience as long as you can still do the job and can dig out evidence to prove it. This is called **APL (accrediting prior learning)** and is one way of collecting evidence quickly.

PERFORMANCE CRITERIA 1.3

(a) I have been at Fareport for five months and have continually
     worked at developing a good working relationship with my
     colleagues. The person I work most closely with is Zena
     Payne. I also deal with the bank and sponsors outside
     Fareport as well as trainers and co-ordinators at Fareport. I
     get on very well with all the people I have contact with.

(b) Fareport have regular meetings on a formal basis to monitor
     how we deliver our training service. I also have informal
     meetings with those I work most closely with to discuss and
     evaluate progress and networks. I use an FTO2 Report
     Form to detail any changes which Zena Payne and I look at
     together.

(c) I deal with the bank and sponsors on a regular basis. This is
     usually by telephone and I back the conversation up by
     writing if necessary. In-house I use face-to-face, written and
     telephone methods of communicating with my colleagues
     (see witness statement).

(d) I am about to begin a new role within Fareport's organisation
     and I am also working towards an assessor award. I have to
     contact the relevant statutory and regulatory bodies including
     RSA and LCCI. All the staff at Fareport are encouraged to
     read any new information and are actively encouraged to
     make new contact if it will benefit our customers, i.e.
     trainees.

(e) Because of the closeness of the staff team the networks I
     described are accurately used to evaluate new ideas. Fareport
     have been awarded the Investors in People Award and as a
     staff team we need to discuss and evaluate new ideas all the
     time.

     Signed........................   Date:.................

Fig. 28. Performance criteria layout.

Range statements
You will need to describe how you have covered the performance criteria for each Element. As you write the descriptions make sure you cover all the range statements.

Check carefully on the 'Evidence Requirements' section as not all the range have to be covered on all the Elements. However, if any of the range haven't been covered you will need to **arrange for additional training or work experience**.

See Figure 28 for an example of how to set out your performance criteria descriptions.

Simulations
A simulated situation (one that is made up to show you can do something) **must not be used** for this Award. If you haven't covered any of the Range you may have to talk to your supervisor and arrange a short job-change to get the experience.

Knowledge
This section is for you to show you have a good knowledge about your company and how to serve customers, including company standards, ways to communicate with customers, rules and regulations, health and safety, etc.

One way to cover this section is to explain your understanding of each point. Use this method of reporting for the 'understanding' section as well.

Understanding
To deal with unexpected as well as expected situations you should have a general understanding of how to handle people, how to behave, what forms to use, how to build good working relationships, etc.

Report these details as for 'knowledge'.

Being observed
A trained assessor will have to watch you doing the job and should give you a record of their observation. People you work with may give you a witness statement to show they believe you are capable. Figures 29 and 30 give examples of each of these very important pieces of evidence.

HOW TO WRITE CASE STUDIES

I want to tell you a story
Think of a case study as telling a story:

FAREPORT TRAINING ORGANISATION LTD

NVQ IN CUSTOMER SERVICE LEVEL III

Candidate: ...Jane Smith............. Centre No: .HGOS 3

Observation from: ....18.3.9-........ To: ...15.9.9-.......

RECORD OF OBSERVATION

UNIT 1   MAINTAIN RELIABLE CUSTOMER SERVICE

Performance Criteria	Summary of Observation
1.3	WORK WITH OTHERS TO BENEFIT THE CUSTOMER
a.	I have observed Jane throughout her five months at Fareport and can confirm she continually and consistently seeks ways to improve her working relationships with myself and the other members of staff.
b.	She works closely with me in my role as Financial Administrator and regularly discusses ways to give a better service to our customers. From our discussions she has produced several new forms and procedures to improve the systems.
c.	When Jane has a query or needs to communicate with the bank or sponsors I have observed her and can confirm she has a good rapport with them. She has recently been in contact with one of our Awarding bodies and I have witnessed the telephone call she made. I can confirm she works very hard to maintain a good flow of information to others outside of the company.
d.	Jane has now moved to the Training and Development Advisor's office and has to make new contacts as a regular task. She has already made contacts with new sponsors who are an important part of our work as they give our trainees the chance to get work experience.
e.	Part of Jane's new role is to look at ideas to improve the way we deliver training and finding placements for our trainees. She works as part of the TDA team and I have observed her actively using different methods to improve the reliability of Fareport.

Range covered? ....Date: 15-9-9

Assessor sig: .... Candidate sig: ....

Fig. 29. Record of observation.

Fareport Training Organisation Ltd

Training Centre, Mill Lane, Gosport PO12 4QG
Tel: 01329 825805

WITNESS STATEMENT

Name of Candidate: Jane Smyth Award: Customer Service III

Name of Witness: Zena Payne

Status of Witness: Financial Manager

Witness employment details:
Fareport Training Organisation

I am Jane's Manager and since joining Fareport five months ago she has worked as a valuable member of the staff team to benefit our customers. She has now been given the opportunity to train as an assessor and has easily taken to her new role.

Since her induction to the role of Training and Development Advisor she has been in contact with relevant statutory and regulatory bodies, ie, the Awarding Bodies, as well as other relevant external suppliers.

I have read the standards for Element 1.3 and can happily confirm she has met all the performance criteria and the Range.

Signature of witness: .... Date: 12.8.9-

Signature of candidate: ....

Fig. 30. Witness statement.

CASE STUDY – ELEMENT 1.3

Between 14 August 1989 and 31 May 1995 I worked for British Gas Plc as a Trainee Showroom Manager based in various showrooms throughout the Portsmouth district.

It was difficult to pre-plan and customers rarely kept set patterns. Often we were overwhelmed with customers. My case study involves an incident during one of these busy periods.

I had taken several 30-minute lunch breaks the previous week as lunch-time is a busy period. I was owed two hours which I booked to take as an early day on Saturday. Late afternoons are usually quiet so this wasn't a problem.

However, at about 3.15 pm one of the staff, Pauline, became involved in a complicated sale. A part-time member of staff (Angela – manning the cash desk) was getting ready to bank up when she found an error of approximately £100.00. I was watching the showroom when she asked me to double-check her money. I did this while she took over my duties. I managed to find the £100 but it took me some time – it was now 4.30 pm.

For me it was standard practice in our showroom to help and assist other colleagues and customers when the need arose. Both my manager and I considered it a vital part of our overall customer service.

Signed:............................... Date: ....

Fig. 31. Case study.

SUMMARY OF EVIDENCE GRID   UNIT 1.3   Make use of networks

Evid. No	Description of Evidence	(a)	(b)	(c)	(d)	(e)	1a	1b	1c	2a	2b	3a	3b	4a	4b	4c	A	B	C	D	E	F	G	H
18	Fareport Organisation Chart					✓	✓	✓	✓									✓	✓		✓			
19	Fareport Job Chart					✓	✓	✓	✓	✓								✓	✓		✓			
20	Fareport Network Flow Chart			✓		✓	✓	✓	✓	✓			✓				✓	✓	✓		✓			
21	British Gas - Network Flow Chart			✓			✓	✓✓	✓	✓✓	✓✓✓		✓				✓	✓✓	✓		✓			
23	Observation	✓	✓✓✓	✓	✓	✓	✓	✓✓	✓	✓	✓	✓	✓	✓		✓	✓✓	✓	✓	✓	✓	✓	✓
11	Witness Statement - L. Crossland	✓				✓		✓	✓					✓✓			✓✓	✓✓		✓✓	✓	✓	✓
10	Witness Statement - 2 Payro		✓			✓		✓	✓				✓	✓			✓✓	✓		✓	✓	✓	-
3	Witness Statement - A Plumbley	✓	✓			✓		✓						✓✓	✓		✓✓✓✓	✓✓	✓	✓✓	✓	✓	✓
7	Witness Statement - Teresa Week	✓				✓		✓	✓						✓		✓✓	✓		✓✓	✓	✓	✓
22	Performance Criteria	✓	✓	✓	✓	✓	✓	✓		✓	✓			✓	✓✓	✓	✓	✓						

Name and Signature of Candidate: ..... JANE SMYTH ......   Date: .... 18·9·9 – ....

Name and Signature of Assessor: ..... LISSA ROE. ......   Date: .... 18·9·9 – ....

Fig. 32. Summary of evidence.

- Introduce the main characters.
- Explain the situation.
- Describe your part.
- Say what happened.
- End by explaining how the situation/problem was resolved.

(See Figure 31 for an example.)

WAYS OF RECORDING EVIDENCE

Evidence of competence
Each awarding body has its own paperwork and you must use what is issued. To give yourself an additional, at-a-glance way to check you have covered everything, use the example in Figure 32 as a summary of your evidence.

Index
As you collect your evidence write the details down. Give each one a number – it doesn't have to be fancy: 1, 2, 3, etc. is good enough. (See Figure 33.)

Use the index to help you cross-reference (using one piece of evidence for more than one element).

ASSESSING AND INTERNALLY VERIFYING YOUR WORK

Someone will have to check your work and this is the job of the Assessor. They have to make sure you have covered all the details in the standards.

An Internal Verifier checks the Assessor has done the job properly. By the time your work is checked by an outside (External) verifier from the Awarding Body it should be to the correct standard and you should receive your certificate.

APPEALS PROCEDURE

When you're being assessed by the Assessor it is possible they may say you're not ready to go on to the next stage. If you feel you are – and are sure you have covered everything – you can insist on being put forward for outside testing. If the assessor still turns you down you can appeal against their decision.

Figure 34 contains a flow chart to show the line of appeal if you feel you are being unjustly treated. Hopefully you won't need to go to these lengths and you will have a good working relationship with your assessor.

Customer Service 3 – Evidence Index

1.1.
1.   Memo – suggestions for timesheet records
2.   Memo – confirming the above
3.   Witness Statement – Ann Plumbley (Manager)
4.   Timesheet checklist
5.   Timesheet instruction sheet
6.   Index box information card
7.   Witness Statement – Teresa Woods
8.   Performance criteria
9.   Assessor observations
1.2
10. Witness Statement – Zena Payne
11. Witness Statement – Lyn Crossland
12. Case Study – service problem
13. Case Study – hours
14. Personal Report – pre-planning
15. FTO2 Report form – trainee cover
16. Performance criteria
17. Assessor observations
1.3
18. Fareport organisational chart
19. Fareport flow chart – Wages Administrator
20. Fareport flow chart – Training and Development Advisor
21. British Gas flow chart
22. Performance criteria
23. Assessor observations

Fig. 33. Index of evidence.

CHECKLIST – EVIDENCE REQUIREMENTS

This following checklist covers what the Award examiner expects to find in your evidence file.

- Curriculum Vitae (outline of your career).
- Description of your job role.
- Award Body paperwork (transcripts, claims to competence, etc.).
- Evidence grids.
- A variety of evidence showing what was done in the workplace and how it was done.
- Proof you can perform a variety of jobs to a consistent standard over a period of time.
- A qualified assessor's 'Record of Observation' as proof they've watched you at work.

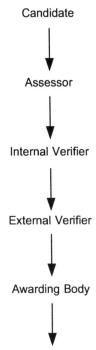

Candidate

Assessor

Internal Verifier

External Verifier

Awarding Body

National Council for Vocational Qualifications

1. All candidates should be aware of the existence of the Appeals Procedure and what action they need to take.

2. All candidates' complaints will be acknowledged and investigated to establish the facts and evidence. When the complaint is justified, action will be taken to rectify its cause.

3. All candidates who register an appeal will receive a formal reply. It is intended that the response will be to the mutual satisfaction of the candidate and the Awarding Body.

4. The operation of the appeals procedure, and results arising from it, will be subject to monitoring to inform future policy.

Fig. 34. Appeals procedure.

Appendix
Checklists for Customer Service
Levels 2 and 3

The following checklists cover units issued by the lead body for Customer Service. They are nationally recognised standards, and qualifications are based on skill and ability to do a job (National Vocational Qualification = NVQ). Examining bodies such as the London Chamber of Commerce, Royal Society of Arts, Pitman, City and Guilds, etc. use them as their guidelines.

The checklists may use words you don't understand. Some of these can be found in the Glossary on page 181 with an explanation of their meaning. You may need to check a dictionary for others not listed.

SUMMARY

Customer Service Level 2
Operate service delivery systems for customers
1.1 Deliver products or services to customers
1.2 Maintain service when systems go wrong
1.3 Maintain positive working relationships with colleagues

Store, retrieve and supply information
2.1 Maintain an established storage system
2.2 Supply information for a specific purpose

Develop and maintain positive working relationships with customers
3.1 Present positive personal image to customer
3.2 Balance needs of customer and organisation
3.3 Respond to feelings expressed by the customer
3.4 Adapt methods of communication to the customer

Solve problems for customers
4.1 Gather information on customer problems
4.2 Propose solutions for customers
4.3 Take action to deliver solutions

Improve service reliability for customers
5.1 Respond promptly to the service needs of customers
5.2 Use customer feedback to improve service reliability
5.3 Work with others to improve service reliability

Customer Service Level 3
Maintain reliable customer service
1.1 Maintain records relating to customer service
1.2 Organise own work pattern to respond to the needs of customers
1.3 Work with others to benefit the customer

Communicate with customers
2.1 Select information for communication to customer
2.2 Improve the flow of information between organisation and customer
2.3 Adapt methods of communication to customer

Develop positive working relationships with customers
3.1 Respond to the needs and feelings expressed by the customer
3.2 Present positive personal image to customer
3.3 Balance the needs of customer and organisation

Solve problems on behalf of customers
4.1 Identify and interpret problems affecting customers
4.2 Generate solutions on behalf of customers
4.3 Take action to deliver solutions

Initiate and evaluate change to improve service to customers
5.1 Obtain and analyse feedback from customers
5.2 Propose improvements in service delivery based on customer feedback
5.3 Initiate changes in response to customer requirements
5.4 Evaluate changes designed to improve service to customers

CUSTOMER SERVICE LEVEL 2

Element 1.1 Delivery products or services to customers

Standard to aim for	*Can you. . .? Do you know. . .?*
Products or services of the organisation are promptly supplied when asked for.	Procedures and policies relating to products or services?
Other products and services are suggested to meet customers' needs.	Relevant products and services provided by organisation?
Customer product or service needs are explored through sensitive questioning.	Questioning and listening techniques?
Own knowledge of products or services is continually updated by using organisational information.	Customers' legal rights?
	How to deliver products and services for customers in a way they understand and appreciate?
	How to keep up-to-date with product or service changes?

Element 1.2 Maintain service when systems go wrong

Standard to aim for	*Can you. . .? Do you know. . .?*
Reasons for failures to service supply are explained to customers immediately.	Statutory and organisational obligations in relation to emergencies and service failure?
Customers are kept updated about interruptions in service.	Sorts of things that could go wrong with service supply in the organisation?
Information given to customers is designed to protect them from unnecessary worry.	Communication channels relating to systems going wrong?
Service is maintained through unprompted extra efforts.	What and how to communicate effectively with customers?
Practical help is offered to colleagues to maintain service to customers when systems go wrong.	How to use own knowledge to maintain service?
	How to use knowledge of others to maintain service?
	How to take initiative whilst still obeying procedures?

Element 1.3 Maintain positive working relationships with colleagues

Standard to aim for	*Can you...? Do you know...?*
Practical help is offered to colleagues under pressure in order to deliver service to customers. Own knowledge of products or services is continually updated through positive exchanges with colleagues. Opportunities to improve working relationships with colleagues are consistently sought. Own knowledge and experience of service systems is shared with others. Co-operative work with others is used to deliver service to customers.	Organisational policy and procedures relating to service delivery? Knowledge of products or services within own area of responsibility? Communication channels within the organisation? How to implement service procedures and policies? How to use own service knowledge in a positive way with others? How to work co-operatively with others?

Element 2.1 Maintain an established storage system

Standard to aim for	*Can you...? Do you know...?*
New information is put into the storage system following organisation procedures. Stored material is maintained in good condition in the appropriate location. Item movements are monitored and recorded accurately. Overdue items are identified and systems for return implemented. Out-of-date information is dealt with as directed. Opportunities for improving established systems are identified and appropriate action taken. Work practices confirm to organisational requirements.	Information classification? Sorting, handling and storing information? Indexing and cross-referencing systems? Storage systems? Control mechanisms? Tracing systems? Procedures and systems of organisation? Security and confidentiality policies? Reporting procedures? Relevant legal requirements? Company and statutory retention policies?

Element 2.2 Supply information for a specific purpose

Standard to aim for	*Can you...? Do you know...?*
Information requirements are understood.	Interpretation of instructions?
Information sources are correctly identified and accessed.	Planning and organising searches?
Where available information does not match requirements,options and alternatives are identified and offered.	Searching for, identifying, accessing and interpreting information?
Information is correctly transcribed and compiled.	Effective use of language – spelling, composition, punctuation, précis?
The information supplied is in an appropriate form.	Presentation of information pictorially, graphically, numerically and textually?
Essential information is supplied within required deadlines.	Location of information?
Confidential information is disclosed only to authorised persons.	Organisation's procedures for accessing information?
	Copyright regulations?
	Security/confidentiality policies?

Element 3.1 Present positive personal image to customer

Standard to aim for	*Can you...? Do you know...?*
Treatment of customers is always courteous and helpful especially when working under pressure.	Organisation's service standards and code of practice?
Organisational standards for personal appearance and behaviour are consistently maintained.	Organisation's standards for appearance and behaviour?
Equipment and supplies used in transactions with customers are available, up-to-date and in good order.	Procedures for the storage, safety, display, maintenance and replacement of equipment and supplies in own area of responsibility?
Opportunities for improving working relationships with customers are actively sought.	Relevant legislation and regulations relating to work with customers?
Own behaviour consistently conveys a positive image of the organisation to current and potential customers, and to colleagues.	How to manage stressful situations?
	How to apply relevant legislation relating to people and equipment?
	How to set an example of positive behaviour for others?
	Ways of creating opportunities to enhance working relationships with customers?

Element 3.2 Balance needs of customer and organisation

Standard to aim for	Can you...? Do you know...?
Determined attempts to meet customer needs are made within own limits of authority.	Relevant products or services of the organisation?
Organisational limitations are explained clearly and positively to the customer.	Procedures for storage, security and confidentiality of records?
	Organisation service standards and code of practice?
All possible actions are taken to minimise conflict between customer needs and organisation limitations.	Formal and informal communication routes?
	Ways of involving others in meeting customer needs?
Organisational limitations are recognised and assistance sought from others.	How to use formal and informal methods to satisfy customer needs within the resources available?
Outcomes of proposals put to customers are clearly recorded and stored in the appropriate place.	When to seek assistance and when to use own initiative?

Element 3.3 Respond to feelings expressed by the customer

Standard to aim for	Can you...? Do you know?....
Customers' feelings are accurately judged through their behaviour, tone, and through sensitive questioning.	Your organisation's service standards and code of practice?
	Your organisation's complaints procedures?
Customers' feelings are acknowledged and own behaviour adapted accordingly.	Relevant products or services relating to your own area of responsibility?
Perceptions of customers' feelings are regularly checked with customer.	Techniques for responding to customer feelings?
Relevant procedures are operated to respond to customer complaints.	How to adapt your own behaviour to respond positively to the feelings of the customer?

Element 3.4 Adapt methods of communication to the customer

Standard to aim for	Can you...? Do you know...?
Appropriate types of communication are selected to keep customers informed about current or future actions. Written and spoken language is suited to the customer. Methods of communication are suited to customers with individual needs. Understanding of communication is regularly checked with customer. Communication difficulties are openly acknowledged and appropriate help is sought to resolve them.	Forms of verbal and non-verbal communication used in working with customers? Other colleagues able to assist in communication with customers with specific individual needs? Procedures for keeping customers informed? Selecting what and when to tell customers about ongoing service issues? How to sense – and get right – different ways of 'getting through' to customers? How to check understanding with customers by 'reading' a variety of signals from them? Ways of seeking help from others to resolve communication difficulties?

Element 4.1 Gather information on customer problems

Standard to aim for	Can you...? Do you know...?
Customer's perceptions of problems are accurately identified and sensitively acknowledged. Customer's problems are clearly summarised using information gained from them. Colleagues are consulted for information relating to problem affecting customers. Recurring problems or complaints are recorded and passed to those who are in a position to provide solutions to them.	Information on relevant products or service relating to customer problems? Relevant legislation relating to service problems? Communication techniques relating to customer problems? Techniques for recording information on customer problems? Choosing the best method of collecting and summarising information? Presenting customer perceptions of problems in an unbiased manner? How to gather information effectively from colleagues?

Element 4.2 Propose solutions for customers

Standard to aim for	Can you. . .? Do you know. . .?
Assistance is sought from colleagues for solutions to customer problems. Current organisational procedures are examined for solutions to customer problems. Other products or services are proposed to solve customer problems. Proposals, and reasons for them, are understood by customers.	Relevant product or service knowledge? Relevant legislation relating to service problems? Organisational procedures relating to service problems? Communication techniques? Ways of working with colleagues to provide solutions to customer problems? Using product or service knowledge to propose solutions to customer problems? How to effectively use own and others' knowledge and experience to propose solutions acceptable to the customer?

Element 4.3 Take action to deliver solutions

Standard to aim for	Can you. . .? Do you know. . .?
Procedures are promptly activated to deliver solutions to customer problems. Service delivery is checked and problems arising are passed to the appropriate authority. Solutions to customer problems are carried out in co-operation with others. Action is taken, within own area of authority, to prevent shortfalls in the delivery of products or services. Action is taken to alert colleagues to potential shortfalls in the delivery of products or services.	Those organisations procedures designed to solve customer problems? Information about relevant products or services relating to customer problems? Communication techniques relating to solution of customer problems? Organisation's checking systems in relation to solving customer service problems? How to use formal and informal procedures to solve problems for customers? How to influence others to deliver solutions to customer problems? Ways of checking service is being delivered effectively?

Element 5.1. Respond promptly to the service needs of customers

Standard to aim for	*Can you. . .? Do you know. . .?*
Customer service needs are identified promptly and clearly.	Organisation service standards and code of practice?
Delays are avoided through unprompted extra efforts.	Organisation complaints procedures and statutory customer rights?
Current procedures are used flexibly to respond to the service needs of customers.	Relevant products or services of the organisation relating to reliable service?
Practical help is gained from others to respond to the service needs of customers.	Sources of assistance outside own area of authority?
	How to judge the expectations of individual customers and how to meet or exceed them?
	Ways of using current procedures flexibly for the benefit of both organisation and customer?
	How to influence others to improve service reliability?

Element 5.2. Use customer feedback to improve service reliability

Standard to aim for	*Can you. . .? Do you know. . .?*
Comments on service reliability are consistently sought from customers.	Organisation's customer feedback procedures?
Existing customer feedback procedures are actively used and outcomes reported regularly to the appropriate authority.	Recording and storing feedback relating to service reliability?
Improvements to service reliability are initiated within own area of authority, as a result of customer feedback.	Procedures for confidentiality and security of information?
Colleagues are informed of service reliability improvements based on customer feedback data.	Complaints procedures relating to own area of responsibility?
	Ways of analysing customer data for use by self and others?
	Ways of improving service reliability based on customer feedback data?

Element 5.3 Work with others to improve service reliability

Standard to aim for	*Can you...? Do you know...?*
Ideas and experience of colleagues are used to improve own service reliability.	Information about relevant products or services in own area of responsibility?
Improvements within own area of responsibility are communicated to others.	Relevant organisational policies and procedures relating to own area of responsibility?
Current organisational procedures for service delivery are regularly evaluated with colleagues.	Relevant legislation relating to service reliability?
Action is taken to alert others to changes needed to improve service reliability.	Team work techniques?
Outcomes of collaborative work with others are actively used to improve service reliability.	How to recognise and use the service improvements of others?
	How to offer ideas and experience to others in a way that they appreciate?
	Ways of working effectively in a team?

CUSTOMER SERVICE LEVEL 3

Element 1.1 Maintain records relating to customer service

Standard to aim for	*Can you...? Do you know...?*
Documentation is comprehensive, correct in detail and contains relevant facts.	What customer service feedback documentation exists?
Facts are set out clearly and concisely.	Information about relevant products or services detailed in records?
Records are regularly and accurately checked, updated and corrected.	Method of storing and retrieving service records?
Suggestions for the improvement of record systems are based on customer needs.	Legal requirements relating to the Data Protection Act?
Suggestions for the improvement of record systems relating to customer service are delivered to the appropriate authority.	How to record information clearly and accurately? How to tell the difference between those records which relate to customer service and those which don't?
Records which can be used to monitor service delivery are clearly identified.	Demonstrating an understanding of what information to document in records and what to leave out and why?
Records can be retrieved easily by others.	How to devise suggestions for improvements to service records which clearly respond to customer need?
Records conform to relevant statutory obligations and requirements regarding confidentiality.	

Element 1.2 Organise own work pattern to respond to the needs of customers

Standard to aim for	*Can you...? Do you know...?*
Advice is sought when limits of own authority and competence are recognised.	Relevant work schedules of the organisation applying to own work role?
Practical help is sought assertively to maintain service to customers during peaks in own workload.	Work priorities of the organisation applying to own workload?
Practical help is offered to colleagues to maintain service to customers during their workload peaks.	Limits of own authority?
Delays are avoided through unprompted extra efforts.	Events likely to cause delays internally and externally?
Positive responses are made to meet abnormal and unexpected workloads.	How own work affects colleagues?
Plans to meet the known demands of future workloads reflect the benefits of experience.	How own work is affected by colleagues?
Own ideas and experience respond sensitively to team and customer needs.	How to maintain working relationships during workload peaks?
	Why workloads elsewhere can adversely affect customer service and how own work can be adjusted to maintain service?
	Ways of influencing others with own ideas and experience?

Element 1.3 Work with others to benefit the customer

Standard to aim for	*Can you. . .? Do you know. . .?*
Opportunities to improve working relationships with colleagues are consistently sought. Current organisational procedures for monitoring service delivery are regularly evaluated with colleagues. Communications with relevant outside parties are effectively maintained on behalf of customers. New contacts likely to benefit customer service are routinely identified through routine scanning of relevant information. Collaborative work with others is actively used to improve the reliability of service delivery.	Relevant suppliers, internal and external? Relevant statutory and regulatory bodies and their effect on customer service? Organisational policy and procedures relating to service delivery? Finding new ways of working with others which benefit the customer? Influencing colleagues to sustain the improved reliability of customer service? How to use new contacts to improve the reliability of customer service? Working with others in ways that they respect and appreciate? How legislation can affect customer service?

Element 2.1 Select information for communication to customer

Standard to aim for	*Can you...? Do you know...?*
Relevant documentation is routinely examined for information relevant to customers.	Information about relevant products or services applying to own work role?
Customers' perception of problems are accurately identified, checked and acknowledged in all communications.	Procedures for security and confidentiality of information applying to own work role?
Information given in response to a wide variety of customer requests meets their needs in terms of accuracy, relevance, promptness and completeness.	Organisational storage and retrieval systems? Where information is kept and how it is accessed? How to sift, store and retrieve information relevant to customers and potential customers?
Customers are told about products or services which meet their identified needs.	How to match available information to individual customer needs?
Information given to customers is presented in a way which minimises worry.	Determining how information selected is the most appropriate for customers?
Information of potential use to customers is stored in the appropriate place.	What to tell and what to hold back from customers whilst still maintaining honesty and integrity?

Element 2.2 Improve the flow of information between organisation and customer

Standard to aim for	*Can you...? Do you know....?*
Information is both given to and drawn from customers to assist progress towards meeting the needs of customers with a timescale acceptable to them.	The formal and informal channels of communication applying to own work role?
Communication optimises the customer's time.	Statutory obligations in regard to information supplied to customers?
Existing opportunities and procedures for communicating with customers are promptly used.	Procedures for security and confidentiality of information?
New opportunities for communicating with customers are developed and used on appropriate occasions.	Information about relevant products or services applying to own work role?
Identified customer problems are discussed with colleagues who are in a position to influence potential solutions.	How to focus sensitively on key issues during exchange with customers?
	What forms of communications to use and when and with whom to use them?
	How to improve the flow of information internally and externally?
	Ways of building an effective two-way relationship with colleagues?

Element 2.3 Adapt methods of communication to customer

Standard to aim for	*Can you...? Do you know...?*
Appropriate communication media are selected to keep customers informed about current or future actions. Written and spoken language is suited to the customer. Methods of communication are suited to customers with individual needs. Understanding of communication is regularly checked with customer. Communication difficulties are openly acknowledged and appropriate help is sought to resolve them.	Forms of verbal and non-verbal communication used in communicating with customers? Other colleagues able to assist in communicating with customers with specific individual needs? Procedures for keeping customers informed? Selecting what and when to tell customers about ongoing service issues? How to sense – and get right – different ways of 'getting through' to customers? How to check understanding with customers by 'reading' a variety of signals from them? Ways of seeking help from others to resolve communication difficulties?

Element 3.1 Respond to the needs and feelings expressed by the customer

Standard to aim for	*Can you...? Do you know...?*
Customers' needs are identified promptly, clearly and sensitively.	Information about relevant products or services?
Customers' feelings are accurately gauged through observation of their behaviour and tone, and through sensitive questioning.	Questioning techniques relating to the needs and feelings of customers?
Own behaviour is always adapted to the perceived needs and feelings of the customer.	Ways in which customers express their feelings?
Perceptions of customers' needs and feelings are regularly checked with customer.	Techniques for responding to customer needs and feelings?
	How to use a range of techniques to identify customer needs?
	How to sense the subtleties of how people feel and respond appropriately to customer?
	How to adapt own behaviour to different customer situations?
	How to use sensitive ways of obtaining feedback from customers about their needs and feelings?

Element 3.2 Present positive personal image to customer

Standard to aim for	*Can you. . .? Do you know. . .?*
Treatment of customers is always courteous and helpful especially when own circumstances are under stress.	Organisation's service standards and code of practice?
Standards for appearance and behaviour are consistently maintained.	Organisation's standards for appearance and behaviour?
Equipment and supplies used in transactions with customers are available, up-to-date and in good order.	Procedures for equipment storage, safety, maintenance and replacement?
Opportunities for improving working relationships with customers are actively sought.	Relevant aspects of the Health and Safety at Work (1974) legislation?
Own behaviour consistently conveys a positive image of the organisation to current and potential customers.	How to manage stressful situations?
	How to apply relevant legislation relating to people and equipment?
	How to set an example of positive behaviour for others?
	Ways of capturing opportunities to enhance internal and external relationships?

Element 3.3 Balance the needs of customer and organisation

Standard to aim for	*Can you. . .? Do you know. . .?*
Persistent attempts are made to meet customer needs.	Information about relevant products or services?
Options for mutual gain are identified and all relevant parties are clearly informed.	Relevant legislation relating to customers and the organisation?
Options for mutual gain are cost-effective for both parties.	Procedures for security and confidentiality of records?
Organisational limitations are explained clearly and positively to the customer.	Possible areas of deviation from service standards and codes of practice?
All possible actions are taken to minimise conflict between customer needs and organisational limitations.	Procedures for storage of records? Ways of responding to customer needs which go beyond normal practice?
Flexibility in organisational limitations is thoroughly explored and own proposals confirmed with others.	Ways of working with others to respond to customer needs? What guidelines to use flexibly and when?
Outcomes of proposals put to customers are clearly recorded, stored and relayed to the appropriate personnel.	Ways of explaining sensitively, yet clearly, the limitations of the organisation? How to satisfy customer needs which challenge current guidelines but are still cost-effective?

Element 4.1 Identify and interpret problems affecting customers

Standard to aim for	Can you...? Do you know...?
Customers' perceptions of problems are accurately identified and sensitively acknowledged. Information relevant to the customers' problems is gathered and systematically analysed and prioritised. Customers' problems are clearly summarised using perceptions and information gained from them. Responses are designed to protect customers from unnecessary worry.	Information on relevant products or services relating to customer problems? Relevant legislation relating to customer problems? Communication techniques relating to customer problems? Analytical procedures relating to customer problems? Ways of collecting, analysing and prioritising information – both quantitative and qualitative? Methods of summarising problems both inside and outside the organisation in a manner that facilitates co-operation? Presenting customer perceptions of problems in an unbiased manner? How to minimise customer anxiety when responding to them about their perceived problems?

Element 4.2 Generate solutions on behalf of customers

Standard to aim for	*Can you...? Do you know...?*
All relevant complaints procedures are examined for solutions to customer problems.	Relevant product or service knowledge relating to the generation of solutions for customers?
Advice is sought from all relevant sources for effective solutions to customer problems.	Relevant legislation relating to the generation of solutions for customers?
Current procedures are flexibly interpreted to generate solutions which benefit customers.	Communication techniques relating to the generation of solutions for customers?
Alternative solutions are identified which benefit the customer.	Ways of generating customer solutions which go beyond normal practice?
Potential new procedures are identified, explored and agreed with appropriate colleagues.	Ways of working with others to solve customer problems which go beyond normal practice?
	What guidelines to use flexibly and when?
	Generating sustainable solutions which benefit both organisation and customer?

Element 4.3 Take action to deliver solutions

Standard to aim for	*Can you. . .? Do you know. . .?*
Procedures are promptly activated to solve customer problems.	Those organisation procedures designed to solve customer problems?
Clear information about recurring problems and complaints is promptly passed to targeted individuals.	Information about relevant products or services relating to the delivery of solutions?
Clear information about effective solutions is promptly passed to targeted individuals.	Communication techniques relating to the delivery of solutions?
Delivery of solution is monitored and suitably modified to resolve any problems arising.	Organisation's customer service monitoring systems?
Appropriate media are used in all communications with customers.	Alternative sources of assistance for customers?
Alternative solutions are presented positively to the customer	How to use standard and non-standard procedures to solve problems for customers?
Accurate advice is given to customers of relevant alternative sources of assistance outside the organisation.	

Element 5.1 Obtain and analyse feedback from customer

Standard to aim for	*Can you. . .? Do you know. . .?*
Comments on organisational service are consistently sought from customers.	Organisation's customer feedback procedures?
Complaints and commendations from customers are used to analyse and evaluate relevant products or services.	Organisational documentation and storage procedures?
New opportunities are generated to gain customer feedback.	Methods of obtaining and analysing feedback?
Customer feedback is analysed for patterns and themes and results are recorded and understood by others.	Ways of gaining feedback from customers?
Customer feedback is stored in the most appropriate place.	Ways of marshalling and analysing data and relating it to present products or services?
	How to translate detailed analysis into an overall view?

Element 5.2 Propose improvements in service delivery based on customer feedback

Standard to aim for	Can you...? Do you know...?
Proposed improvements to customer service are clearly presented in the appropriate form and are based on accurate information. Predictions are made about customer requirements based on the accurate interpretation of customer feedback. Concise information which accurately summarises proposed improvements is passed to appropriately targeted individuals.	Information about relevant products or services relating to service improvement? Relevant organisational policies and procedures relating to service improvement? Relevant legislation relating to service improvement? Analytical and presentation techniques relating to proposed improvements? How proposed improvements demonstrate an understanding of organisational policy and procedures? How to summarise proposed changes for different people? How to influence others in relation to proposed changes?

Element 5.3 Initiate changes in response to customer requirements

Standard to aim for	*Can you...? Do you know...?*
Action is taken, within own area of authority, to remedy shortfalls in customer service.	Relevant product or service knowledge relating to changes initiated?
Action is taken to alert others to changes needed to improve customer service.	Relevant organisational policies and procedures relating to changes initiated?
Own initiatives are introduced which respond to customer requirements and are within own area of authority.	Relevant legislation relating to changes initiated?
Actions and initiatives are based on thorough analysis of appropriate data and take account of any predicted customer needs.	Methods of analysing data relating to changes initiated? Communication channels within the organisation?
Own ideas and experience are used to implement changes introduced by others.	Ways of working with others to improve customer service? How to take initiative in improving customer service? How own ideas relate to those of others and the policy of the organisation?

Element 5.4 Evaluate changes designed to improve service to customers

Standard to aim for	*Can you...? Do you know...?*
Outcomes of changes to improve customer service are systematically monitored using all available feedback.	Relevant product or service knowledge relating to the evaluation of change?
Implications of changes to products or services are identified and appropriate colleague(s) are informed.	Relevant organisational policies and procedures relating to the evaluation of change?
Recommendations on the effectiveness of changes designed to improve customer service are communicated to the appropriate colleague(s).	Relevant legislation relating to the evaluation of change?
	Methods of analysing feedback on service improvements?
	Communication channels within the organisation?
	How to identify whether changes have improved service to customers?
	How to identify the future implications of changes?
	How to recommend future effective action?

Useful Addresses

National Council for Vocational Qualifications, 222 Euston Road, London NW1 2BZ.

Awarding bodies
City and Guilds, 46 Britannia Street, London WC1X 9RG.
London Chamber of Commerce, Marlow House, Station Road, Sidcup, Kent DA15 7BJ.
Pitman Examinations Institute, 1 Giltspur Street, London EC1A 9DH.
RSA Examinations Board, Westwood Way, Coventry CV4 8HS.

Other organisations
Trading Standards office (see telephone directory for local county council).
Health and Safety Executive, PO Box 1999, Sudbury, Suffolk CO10 6FS.
The Data Protection Register, Wycliffe House, Water Lane, Wilmslow, Cheshire SK9 5AF.
The British Copyright Council, Copyright House, 29–33 Berners Street, London W1P 4AA.
The Patent Office, Industrial Property and Copyright Department, Copyright Enquiries, Room 1504, State House, 66–71 High Holborn, London WC1R 4TP.

Further Reading

Administration Student Handbook, C. Carysforth and M. Rawlinson (Heinemann).

Business (GNVQ), D. Needham and R. Dransfield (Heinemann).

Communication (GNVQ), M. Waterman and Olivia Rogers (Heinemann).

Competitive Customer Care, M. Stone (Croner).

Customer Care Management, A. Brown (Heinemann).

Customer Service: How to Achieve Total Customer Satisfaction, M. Peel (Kogan Page).

Customer Service Pocket Book, T. Newley (Management Pocket Books).

Golden Rules of Customer Care, C. Sewell (Business Books).

How to Buy and Run a Shop, Iain Maitland (How To Books).

How to Communicate at Work, Ann Dobson (How To Books).

How to Improve Your Customer Service, S. Macaulay (Kogan Page).

How to Manage People at Work, John Humphries (How To Books).

How to Turn Customer Service into Customer Sales, B. Katz (Pitman).

How to Win Customers: Using Customer Service, J. Horowitz (Pitman).

How to Work in an Office, Sheila Payne (How To Books).

How to Work in Retail, Sylvia Lichfield and Christine Hall (How To Books).

Managing Yourself, Julie-Ann Amos (How To Books).

People in Retailing, V. Hughes and D. Weller (Macmillan).

Perfect Customer Care: All Your Need to Get it Right First Time, T. Johns (Arrow).

Glossary

Action plan: a plan detailing which actions need to be tackled. A date for review and completion may be included.

APL: giving credit for past experience.

Approved centre: an organisation which has successfully gained approval to offer NVQs.

Assessor: a person qualified to observe and assess an NVQ candidate's work performance. Should possess D32/D33 Award.

Awarding body: a group or organisation approved by NCVQ to provide NVQ awards, e.g. City and Guilds.

Behaviour: the way in which people react in a given situation.

Body language: gestures and postures which convey a hidden message behind verbal **communication**.

Candidate: a person seeking recognition for their work **competence** in the form of an NVQ.

Communication: the exchange of ideas and information between groups or individuals to achieve a mutual understanding. Can be by word of mouth, by telephone or in writing.

Competence: having the ability to do a job or tasks.

Copyright law: a law designed to stop others from publishing/copying material written/produced by someone else without their permission.

Core skills (now known as 'key skills'): number, communication, problem-solving and practical skills. The basic personal and life skills a candidate needs to develop and use in everyday tasks.

Curriculum vitae: a list of personal details, work experience, qualifications, etc.

Data Protection Act: a law to protect people from having their work copied without consent or their reputation from being harmed by information stored on a computerised data system.

Evaluation: a process to review the result of a decision or solution.

Evidence: proof a **candidate** can do the job. Could include written evidence, an observed performance or a witness statement from qualified colleagues.

External verifier: employed by **awarding bodies** to monitor **assessor/ internal verifier** performance and ensure the NVQ standards are maintained.

Incentive: a reward offered for performing certain tasks or actions.

Internal verifier: in position to internally check an **assessor** is maintaining the national standards for the NVQ. Should possess the D33/D34 Award.

ISO9002: British Standard **quality assurance**. Recognises a standard quality in a company's systems and procedures.

Jargon: language of technical or special words.

Lead body: the main body responsible for setting the standards. These groups are predominantly led by employers in their relevant area of work.

Liaise: to talk or work together with others for a purpose.

Manager: one who leads, motivates and develops others to achieve an agreed objective.

Motivate: to offer the appropriate **incentives** to satisfy people's needs in order to persuade them to undertake tasks and to behave in a required manner.

NCVQ: National Council for Vocational Qualifications. The body responsible for validating/accrediting standards/awards/awarding bodies in England and Wales.

Non-verbal communication: see **body language**.

NVQ: National Vocational Qualification. Qualifications gained by using your work experience as proof of being able to do a competent job.

Observation: the act in which an **assessor** watches a **candidate**'s performance at work.

Performance criteria: a standard on which a judgment or decision may be based when checking for a **candidate**'s competent performance in a job or task.

Portfolio: a folder or file. **Candidate** stores **evidence** of **competence** in a portfolio, sometimes called a 'performance record'.

Qualification: the formal recognition that the defined standard has been achieved.

Quality assurance: guarantee that the quality is being maintained through an agreed process for monitoring or verification of the standard.

Range statement: a statement which describes the range and context of activities to which a specified unit or element of competence applies.

Resources: what a manager has to manage, i.e. people, time, space, etc. Can also be stock items necessary to perform a task.

Self-assessment: a **candidate** can self-assess (assess their own performance) by this process. It encourages them to identify where more training is needed or where the standards have been met.

Standard: the measure of **competence** agreed by the **lead body** which describes what has to be achieved.

Stress: a mental state brought about by excessive pressure of events both at work and at home.

Team: a group of people working together to achieve a specific objective.

Time management: planning to use time in a most effective manner.

Verification: the process of ensuring the standard is being maintained and appropriate systems are in place.

Index

MASTERING BUSINESS ENGLISH
How to sharpen up your business communication skills

Michael Bennie

Are you communicating effectively? Do your business documents achieve the results you want? Or are they too often ignored or misunderstood? Good communication is the key to success in any business. Whether you are trying to sell a product, answer a query or complaint, or persuade colleagues, the way you express yourself is often as important as what you say. With lots of examples, checklists and questionnaires to help you, the new edition of this book will speed you on your way. 'An excellent book—... Altogether most useful for anyone seeking to improve their communication skills.' *IPS Journal.* 'Gives guidance on writing styles for every situation... steers the reader through the principles and techniques of effective letter-writing and document-planning.' *First Voice.* 'Useful chapters on grammar, punctuation and spelling. Frequent questionnaires and checklists enable the reader to check progress.' *Focus (Society of Business Teachers).* 'The language and style is easy to follow...Excellent value for money.' *Spoken English.*

208pp illus. 1 85703 349 3. 3rd edition.

INVESTING IN PEOPLE
How to help your organisation achieve higher standards and a competitive edge

Dr Harley Turnbull

Investors in People is the most important quality programme for change in the 1990s. As Sir Brian Wolfson, Chairman, Investors in People, UK, said (*Employment News,* June 1995), 'Thousands of companies across the country are involved in gaining sustainable, competitive advantage for their business by introducing the winning principles of the Investor in People Standard.' The National Advisors Council for Education and Training Targets has set an Investor in People target for the year 2000: 70% of all organisations employing 200 or more employees and 35% employing 50 or more, to be recognised as Investors in People. Dr Harley Turnbull, a chartered Occupational Psychologist and Member of the Institute of Personnel and Development, has professional experience of IIP both as an internal HRD manager and external consultant.

184pp illus. 1 85703 188 1.

WINNING PRESENTATIONS
How to sell your ideas and yourself

Ghassan Hasbani

'Good communication skills' is a phrase repeatedly used in job descriptions and CVs. These skills can make or break people's careers and are highly regarded by employers and organisations. One of the most important skills is the ability to present and put your ideas across whether you are an employee or an independent consultant, a civil servant or businessperson, a school teacher or a university lecturer, a member of the local club or someone starting a career in politics. No matter who you are or what kind of work you do, you always need to communicate with people on different occasions and present to them ideas, news, or achievements. This step-by-step guide tells you all you need to know in order to become confident in giving effective presentations, that will help you succeed in your life and career. Presenting is not necessarily a gift, it is a skill which can be learned or acquired and this book will help you do that. Ghassan Hasbani started writing and presenting for television at the age of 16. He currently works as a telecommunications engineer, where he uses his skills to present new technologies in seminars and lectures. He also works as a visiting university lecturer teaching management and communication skills to undergraduates.

157pp illus. 1 85703 309 4.

WRITING BUSINESS LETTERS
A practical introduction for everyone

Ann Dobson

Without proper help, lots of people find it quite hard to cope with even basic business correspondence. Intended for absolute beginners, this book uses fictional characters in a typical business setting to contrast the right and wrong ways to go about things. Taking nothing for granted, the book shows how to plan a letter, how to write and present it, how to deal with requests, how to write and answer complaints, standard letters, personal letters, job applications, letters overseas, and a variety of routine and tricky letters. Good, bad and middling examples are used, to help beginners see for themselves the right and wrong ways of doing things. Ann Dobson is principal of a secretarial training school with long experience of helping people improve their business skills.

183pp illus. 1 85703 339 6. 2nd edition.

How To Books

How To Books provide practical help on a large range of topics. They are available through all good bookshops or can be ordered direct from the distributors. Just tick the titles you want and complete the form on the following page.

___ Apply to an Industrial Tribunal (£7.99)
___ Applying for a Job (£8.99)
___ Applying for a United States Visa (£15.99)
___ Backpacking Round Europe (£8.99)
___ Be a Freelance Journalist (£8.99)
___ Be a Freelance Secretary (£8.99)
___ Become a Freelance Sales Agent (£9.99)
___ Become an Au Pair (£8.99)
___ Becoming a Father (£8.99)
___ Buy & Run a Shop (£8.99)
___ Buy & Run a Small Hotel (£8.99)
___ Buying a Personal Computer (£9.99)
___ Career Networking (£8.99)
___ Career Planning for Women (£8.99)
___ Cash from your Computer (£9.99)
___ Choosing a Nursing Home (£9.99)
___ Choosing a Package Holiday (£8.99)
___ Claim State Benefits (£9.99)
___ Collecting a Debt (£9.99)
___ Communicate at Work (£7.99)
___ Conduct Staff Appraisals (£7.99)
___ Conducting Effective Interviews (£8.99)
___ Coping with Self Assessment (£9.99)
___ Copyright & Law for Writers (£8.99)
___ Counsel People at Work (£7.99)
___ Creating a Twist in the Tale (£8.99)
___ Creative Writing (£9.99)
___ Critical Thinking for Students (£8.99)
___ Dealing with a Death in the Family (£9.99)
___ Do Voluntary Work Abroad (£8.99)
___ Do Your Own Advertising (£8.99)
___ Do Your Own PR (£8.99)
___ Doing Business Abroad (£10.99)
___ Doing Business on the Internet (£12.99)
___ Emigrate (£9.99)
___ Employ & Manage Staff (£8.99)
___ Find Temporary Work Abroad (£8.99)
___ Finding a Job in Canada (£9.99)
___ Finding a Job in Computers (£8.99)
___ Finding a Job in New Zealand (£9.99)
___ Finding a Job with a Future (£8.99)
___ Finding Work Overseas (£9.99)
___ Freelance DJ-ing (£8.99)
___ Freelance Teaching & Tutoring (£9.99)
___ Get a Job Abroad (£10.99)
___ Get a Job in America (£9.99)
___ Get a Job in Australia (£9.99)
___ Get a Job in Europe (£9.99)
___ Get a Job in France (£9.99)
___ Get a Job in Travel & Tourism (£8.99)
___ Get into Radio (£8.99)
___ Getting into Films & Television (£10.99)

___ Getting That Job (£8.99)
___ Getting your First Job (£8.99)
___ Going to University (£8.99)
___ Helping your Child to Read (£8.99)
___ How to Study & Learn (£8.99)
___ Investing in People (£9.99)
___ Investing in Stocks & Shares (£9.99)
___ Keep Business Accounts (£7.99)
___ Know Your Rights at Work (£8.99)
___ Live & Work in America (£9.99)
___ Live & Work in Australia (£12.99)
___ Live & Work in Germany (£9.99)
___ Live & Work in Greece (£9.99)
___ Live & Work in Italy (£8.99)
___ Live & Work in New Zealand (£9.99)
___ Live & Work in Portugal (£9.99)
___ Live & Work in the Gulf (£9.99)
___ Living & Working in Britain (£8.99)
___ Living & Working in China (£9.99)
___ Living & Working in Hong Kong (£10.99)
___ Living & Working in Israel (£10.99)
___ Living & Working in Saudi Arabia (£12.99)
___ Living & Working in the Netherlands (£9.99)
___ Making a Complaint (£8.99)
___ Making a Wedding Speech (£8.99)
___ Manage a Sales Team (£8.99)
___ Manage an Office (£8.99)
___ Manage Computers at Work (£8.99)
___ Manage People at Work (£8.99)
___ Manage Your Career (£8.99)
___ Managing Budgets & Cash Flows (£9.99)
___ Managing Meetings (£8.99)
___ Managing Your Personal Finances (£8.99)
___ Managing Yourself (£8.99)
___ Market Yourself (£8.99)
___ Master Book-Keeping (£8.99)
___ Mastering Business English (£8.99)
___ Master GCSE Accounts (£8.99)
___ Master Public Speaking (£8.99)
___ Migrating to Canada (£12.99)
___ Obtaining Visas & Work Permits (£9.99)
___ Organising Effective Training (£9.99)
___ Pass Exams Without Anxiety (£7.99)
___ Passing That Interview (£8.99)
___ Plan a Wedding (£7.99)
___ Planning Your Gap Year (£8.99)
___ Prepare a Business Plan (£8.99)
___ Publish a Book (£9.99)
___ Publish a Newsletter (£9.99)
___ Raise Funds & Sponsorship (£7.99)
___ Rent & Buy Property in France (£9.99)
___ Rent & Buy Property in Italy (£9.99)

How To Books

___ Research Methods (£8.99)	___ Use the Internet (£9.99)
___ Retire Abroad (£8.99)	___ Winning Consumer Competitions (£8.99)
___ Return to Work (£7.99)	___ Winning Presentations (£8.99)
___ Run a Voluntary Group (£8.99)	___ Work from Home (£8.99)
___ Setting up Home in Florida (£9.99)	___ Work in an Office (£7.99)
___ Spending a Year Abroad (£8.99)	___ Work in Retail (£8.99)
___ Start a Business from Home (£7.99)	___ Work with Dogs (£8.99)
___ Start a New Career (£6.99)	___ Working Abroad (£14.99)
___ Starting to Manage (£8.99)	___ Working as a Holiday Rep (£9.99)
___ Starting to Write (£8.99)	___ Working in Japan (£10.99)
___ Start Word Processing (£8.99)	___ Working in Photography (£8.99)
___ Start Your Own Business (£8.99)	___ Working in the Gulf (£10.99)
___ Study Abroad (£8.99)	___ Working in Hotels & Catering (£9.99)
___ Study & Live in Britain (£7.99)	___ Working on Contract Worldwide (£9.99)
___ Studying at University (£8.99)	___ Working on Cruise Ships (£9.99)
___ Studying for a Degree (£8.99)	___ Write a Press Release (£9.99)
___ Successful Grandparenting (£8.99)	___ Write a Report (£8.99)
___ Successful Mail Order Marketing (£9.99)	___ Write an Assignment (£8.99)
___ Successful Single Parenting (£8.99)	___ Write & Sell Computer Software (£9.99)
___ Survive Divorce (£8.99)	___ Write for Publication (£8.99)
___ Surviving Redundancy (£8.99)	___ Write for Television (£8.99)
___ Taking in Students (£8.99)	___ Writing a CV that Works (£8.99)
___ Taking on Staff (£8.99)	___ Writing a Non Fiction Book (£9.99)
___ Taking Your A-Levels (£8.99)	___ Writing an Essay (£8.99)
___ Teach Abroad (£8.99)	___ Writing & Publishing Poetry (£9.99)
___ Teach Adults (£8.99)	___ Writing & Selling a Novel (£8.99)
___ Teaching Someone to Drive (£8.99)	___ Writing Business Letters (£8.99)
___ Travel Round the World (£8.99)	___ Writing Reviews (£9.99)
___ Understand Finance at Work (£8.99)	___ Writing Your Dissertation (£8.99)
___ Use a Library (£7.99)	

To: Plymbridge Distributors Ltd, Plymbridge House, Estover Road, Plymouth PL6 7PZ. Customer Services Tel: (01752) 202301. Fax: (01752) 202331.

Please send me copies of the titles I have indicated. Please add postage & packing (UK £1, Europe including Eire, £2, World £3 airmail).

☐ I enclose cheque/PO payable to Plymbridge Distributors Ltd for £ [_____]

☐ Please charge to my ☐ MasterCard, ☐ Visa, ☐AMEX card.

Account No. [_ _ _ _ _ _ _ _ _ _ _ _ _ _ _]

Card Expiry Date [__] 19   ☎ **Credit Card orders may be faxed or phoned.**

Customer Name (CAPITALS) ....

Address ....

.... Postcode ....

Telephone .... Signature ....

Every effort will be made to despatch your copy as soon as possible but to avoid possible disappointment please allow up to 21 days for despatch time (42 days if overseas). Prices and availability are subject to change without notice.

Code BPA